Twayne's United States Authors Series

EDITOR OF THIS VOLUME

Sylvia E. Bowman

Richard Wright

TUSAS 386

Richard Wright

RICHARD WRIGHT

By ROBERT FELGAR
Jacksonville State University

TWAYNE PUBLISHERS
A DIVISION OF G. K. HALL & CO., BOSTON

Published in 1980 by Twayne Publishers,
A Division of G. K. Hall & Co.

Printed on permanent/durable acid-free paper and bound
in the United States of America

Library of Congress Cataloging in Publication Data

Felgar, Robert, 1944–
Richard Wright.

(Twayne's United States authors series; TUSAS 386)
Bibliography: p. 180-85
Includes index.
1. Wright, Richard, 1908–1960—Criticism and interpretation.
PS3545.R815Z6517 813′.52 80–16309
ISBN 0-8057-7320-7

To Catherine and Donald

Contents

	About the Author	
	Preface	
	Chronology	
1.	An American Son's Life	17
2.	His Apprenticeship	54
3.	His Fulfillment	78
4.	An Exile's Fiction	109
5.	An Exile's Nonfiction	137
6.	*Eight Men*	156
7.	Conclusion	174
	Notes and References	176
	Selected Bibliography	180
	Index	186

About the Author

Robert Felgar, who was born in Indianapolis, Indiana, in 1944, grew up in various parts of the United States, including Texas, Michigan, New York, and California. He received his A.B. in 1966 from Occidental College, his M.A. in 1968, and his Ph.D. in 1970 from Duke University. From 1969-70 he was part-time instructor of English at Duke; during the 1970-71 academic year he was assistant professor of English at Virginia Wesleyan College; since 1971 he has been associate professor of English at Jacksonville State University. He has published in the *Browning Newsletter*, *Studies in Black Literature*, *Browning Society Notes*, *Studies in Browning and His Circle*, *College Language Association Journal*, and *Black American Literature Forum*.

Preface

Richard Wright's fiction is the most powerful that has emerged to date in black literature; and Wright—friend to and influence on Ralph Ellison; father-figure to James Baldwin; a man greatly admired by Eldridge Cleaver—is the virtual father of the explosion of enraged black literary talent that took the stage in the 1960s. His greatness lies not only in having influenced black literature but also in having been perhaps the very first writer to give the white community explanations and themes that cut through its prejudices and forced it to look at the reality of black life in America. Some of his themes we American blacks and whites absorbed readily, though not always eagerly: that the black man is America's metaphor because, in a few hundred years, he has experienced through intense victimization what the white West has suffered in a few thousand years; that against a cosmic setting all men are like blacks in the Bottom South; that black-white relations rest on a peculiar sexual dynamic; and that freedom is the ultimate value.

But the most provoking theme of Wright's, "The secret of race is that there is no secret," has been persistently resisted. For instance and notably, *Native Son*, which deals with Bigger Thomas, a stunted black man who kills two women and goes to his execution ostensibly feeling morally triumphant because of the murders, has caused controversy to rage over the meaning of its ending from the moment of its best-selling publication in 1940. An achievement of my book is to give the final word on the controversy and to demonstrate that Bigger does indeed die as unregenerate as he lived and as worthless as society made him. But the achievement is truly Wright's, not mine; for Wright is so clear, so dispassionate, in setting forth Bigger's sad tale, that it takes simply a careful reading to unlock the book's message once the scales of wish-fulfillment and prejudice drop from the reader's eyes and he comes to see with a vision as undistorted as Wright's that *Native Son* is the story of *any* brutalized and hopeless human, regardless of race. Abused and despised as Bigger was, anyone could become a Bigger Thomas; it is environment, not racial predisposition, that produces human monsters.

Black Boy, too, is most profitably examined from a viewpoint that resists prefabricated theories in an effort to see what the text actually says. There is woe-saying by critics that, because of remarks in Wright's autobiographical masterpiece that are bitterly critical of his black southern community, he lacks racial pride and dignity. My book's "discovery," that Wright is a man proud of himself to the fullest extent, which means, necessarily, that he is also proud of his racial heritage, is once again simply the close reading of *Black Boy* in conjunction with his other manifesto of black experience, *Twelve Million Black Voices*, which deals with Afro-American history. As in *Native Son*, Wright is ahead not only of his time but also ahead of the present day—he feels no racial shame in being critical of his community when he recounts how his life was hampered by black culture any more than he feels self-congratulatory when he limns the great virtues of his race which has persisted not only in surviving, despite unbelievable odds, but has also continued to flourish and grow. To Wright, race is always, simply and unemotively, race: we blacks and whites will have come far when we catch up with his thinking that race involves neither superiority, inferiority, nor mystique.

Nor is it simply truths which are so obvious that they have remained hidden or overexplained that Wright excels in exploring. His intuitive psychological grasp of the phemomena of racism is sometimes startling: my book demonstrates that at least two of the themes set down by Eldridge Cleaver in his monumental *Soul on Ice* were, in fact, anticipated by Wright; both deal with the skewed sexuality that results from racism. But where Cleaver sets the theories down in essay form, then mythically extrapolates from them, Wright leaves the themes unstated but uses them as the dynamics of plot. In *Native Son*, for example, Wright's characters can be divided into four groups that correspond to the four sexual types that Cleaver establishes to explain the bizarre sexuality of racism. And the little-known short story "Big Black Good Man" is illuminated by Cleaver's theory of black homosexuality in a startling way.

One of Wright's triumphs is probably unique in American literature—his successful overcoming of the horrible experiences of the Deep South, which he not only survived but forged into great literary art. This remarkable ability to overcome formidable barriers to literary achievement, whether economic, familial, educational, or racial, is the keynote of much of his writing. "The Ethics of Living Jim Crow" and *Black Boy* render with great power the way Wright's literary imagination was obsessed with his own history. Because his past was always so vividly present to him, and because it determined the shape and quality of so much of his writing, it is heavily emphasized in this study.

Wright's literary themes and triumphs, of course, cannot be separated from his technique, and that technique is not minimized here. His sometimes underestimated literary craftsmanship is discussed at length. No Henry James, he was nevertheless able to exploit impressively the conventions of Realism (in *Uncle Tom's Children*), Naturalism (in *Native Son*), Symbolism (in "The Man Who Was Almost a Man"), and Surrealism (in "The Man Who Lived Underground"). And Wright's sheer literary power, his knack for narrating and dramatizing telling indictments of American and human ideals, receives considerable emphasis in the discussions of "Between the World and Me," "The Ethics of Living Jim Crow," *Uncle Tom's Children*, *Native Son*, and "The Man Who Lived Underground."

Not treated so thoroughly are the less impressive aspects of Wright's corpus. His workmanlike journalism and his negligible poetry, both the Communist propaganda and the *haiku*, do not justify extended discussion. The reporting he did for the *Daily Worker* and *New Masses* reads as if it were dictated by a computer programmed by Marx himself; it is very earnest reporting but utterly predictable. As for his verse, the harsh truth is that, with the exception of "Between the World and Me," and perhaps "We of the Streets," it is poetry only in its appearance on the page. His later novels—*The Outsider*, *Savage Holiday*, *The Long Dream*—do not warrant thorough examination because they compare so utterly unfavorably with *Native Son*. They are read largely because they were written by the author of the latter novel. With the exception of *Black Power*, the travel books and lectures do not invite extensive consideration because they are so often tendentious and filled with sociopolitical posturing.

In order to fulfill the objective of the book, which is the exposition of Wright's themes, ideas, and techniques, its contents are organized, for the most part, in the chronological order in which Wright composed his work. The exceptions are his writing done in the 1950s, which is divided conveniently into fictional and nonfictional categories in Chapters 4 and 5; and his autobiography *Black Boy*, which reflects his frame of mind at the time in his life when he was writing it and is included in the introductory chapter along with *Twelve Million Black Voices*. By examining most of Wright's major writings chronologically, the reader apprehends how his work progressed essentially by his raising the level of abstraction of his own experience in the South; in a sense, everything he wrote is an attempt to convey that experience, whether he was dealing with blacks in the South or in the North, whites in New York City, black Africans in Ghana, Protestants in Spain, or the Third World in Indonesia. And the reader simultaneously watches Wright broaden and diversify his literary strategies in an effort to encompass his widening perspective.

I should like to thank Hannah Hedrick, editor of *Negro American Literature Forum* (now *Black American Literature Forum*), for permission to quote from my article "*Soul on Ice* and *Native Son*," which appeared in the fall 1974 issue; and Therman B. O'Daniel, editor of *College Language Association Journal*, and the College Language Association, for permission to use my article " 'The Kingdom of the Beast': The Landscape of *Native Son*," which appeared in the March 1974 issue. I am also indebted to William Simpson, former librarian at Jacksonville State University, who found many items for me, and to my wife, who read and typed relentlessly.

ROBERT FELGAR

Jacksonville State University

Chronology

1908	Richard Wright born to Ella and Nathan Wright on September 4 on a farm near Natchez, Mississippi.
1910	Brother, Leon, born.
1912	Sets fire to his maternal grandmother's home and then hides under it; this incident, rendered in sensational terms in *Black Boy*, prefigures two of his presiding metaphors—fire and the underground.
1914	Nathan Wright deserts his young family; economic pressures on Mrs. Wright and her two boys become intense. At the age of six, Wright is a drunkard.
1916	Receives his first formal education; Ella becomes ill and he has to take care of her; he drops out of school.
1920	Attends the Seventh-Day Adventist school in Huntsville, Mississippi.
1921	Attends the Jim Hill Public School, where he shows himself to be very bright; threatens to leave home if his maternal grandmother refuses to permit him to work on Saturday, the Adventist Sabbath.
1923	Becomes a student at the Smith-Robinson Public School, where he is also very promising.
1924	First publication, "The Voodoo of Hell's Half Acre," appears in a black newspaper, the *Southern Register* (no copy extant).
1925	Graduates as valedictorian from the Smith-Robinson Public School; resolves to leave the South, not realizing his experience there had permanently shaped his outlook; arrives in Memphis in the fall.
1926	Begins intense reading, his salvation: H. L. Mencken, Sinclair Lewis, Theodore Dreiser.
1927-1928	Goes to Chicago: Up South (he finds the entire country is the South); spends his nights as a postal clerk; during his days he is a reader and a writer.
1929	The Great Depression costs him his job at the post office.

1931 Forced to go on relief, he finds a job in the Michael Reese Hospital, the inspiration for "What You Don't Know Won't Hurt You." The relief office sends him to the South Side Boys' Club, where he sees many Bigger Thomases. In April his second publication, "Superstition," appears in *Abbott's Monthly Magazine*.

1932 Attends meetings of the John Reed Club, a Communist literary organization; begins publishing poems and short stories in leftist journals, *New Masses*, *Left Front*, *International Literature*.

1933 Makes one of the few strong commitments in his life in joining the Communist party.

1936 Publishes one of his finest stories, "Big Boy Leaves Home," in *New Caravan*.

1937 Goes to New York, where he becomes Harlem editor for the *Daily Worker*; his literary reputation begins to grow.

1938 His first published book, *Uncle Tom's Children*, appears; he becomes romantically interested in two women—Dhimah Rose Meadman, a dancer, and Ellen Poplar, a member of the Communist party.

1939 Receives Guggenheim Fellowship; completes *Native Son*, his finest novel; marries Dhimah Rose Meadman.

1940 *Native Son* published; his reputation becomes national. Goes to Mexico with Dhimah; estranged from Dhimah, he returns to New York City by way of the Deep South.

1941 Marries Ellen Poplar. Collaborates with Paul Green on a dramatic version of *Native Son*. *Twelve Million Black Voices* published.

1942 Daughter, Julia, born.

1945 Publication of *Black Boy*, in many ways his best book. Meets James Baldwin.

1946 Visits France, where he feels free for the first time in his life.

1947 Leaves America to reside in France, his home base for the rest of his life, although he travels extensively. Becomes friends with Jean-Paul Sartre and Simone de Beauvoir.

1949 Second daughter, Rachel, born. Makes arrangements for a film version of *Native Son*, with himself as Bigger.

1949-1950 In Argentina for the filming of *Native Son*.

1953 *The Outsider*. Visits the Gold Coast (Ghana), the subject of *Black Power*.

1954 *Black Power*. Also publishes *Savage Holiday*, his only novel with all white characters. Visits Spain.

1955 Attends the Bandung Conference (on Third World problems) in Indonesia.

1956 Publishes *The Color Curtain*: *A Report on the Bandung Conference* and *Pagan Spain*, which is based on his travels in Spain.

1957 *White Man, Listen!*, a collection of lectures.

1958 *The Long Dream* appears as first part of a projected trilogy.

1960 Writes many *haiku* poems. Dies of a heart attack on November 28.

CHAPTER 1

An American Son's Life

IN a relatively brief lifetime, Richard Wright experienced what the white people of the Western world have suffered over a period of several hundred years. Born into a minority culture which was preindividualist,[1] religious, superstitious, agrarian-rural, southern, and often passive, Wright died an agnostic rationalist who was living on the edge of the Western version of reality. Throughout his life he retained, however, many of his childhood values; and he did so even while he was becoming one of the most famous American writers. Moreover, the past which had produced him was always present for him in a fashion that is unique among American writers. His experience obsessed him because he never really accepted it; his writing is the result of this obsession.

Natchez, Mississippi, on September 4, 1908, the date of his birth, was one of the most backward and poor areas of a racist country; the state was so racist, in fact, that accurate records of the birth of black children were not kept. The obstacles placed before black people in Mississippi in the early twentieth century were so formidable that Wright's eventual emergence from the South recapitulates the escape of the Israelites from Pharaoh, for everything was done to keep Wright and his fellow blacks "in their place." His parents had been kept pretty much in theirs: Nathan Wright, the father, was an illiterate sharecropper (a euphemism for "slave") on a plantation—the locus of black culture until the 1920s. Ella, the mother, was a schoolteacher; and therefore, as one in the black middle class, she had married beneath herself.

The birth of a child to a family so undistinguished (though mismatched) naturally received little notice from the world at large; nor is it imaginable that his parents kept a gloating, middle-class, annotated photograph album of their first-born. As a result, little information exists about young Richard except what he has shared with his readers in *Black Boy*, which begins at the age of four, since "Richard remembered little of his first three years."[2] His experience at four, though, was so violent that not only did it engrave itself on his mind, but it also allowed him to forge one of the most dramatically intense openings in all his writing—one rivaled by nothing else but the first pages of *Native Son*—the occurrence was Richard's setting his house on fire.

He had spent a bored and fretful afternoon under the stricture to keep quiet so that he would not bother his maternal grandmother, who was ill. When the fire in the fireplace attracted his irritable attention, he considered throwing his picture book into it (the picture book is one piece of evidence among many that his upbringing was more middle class, by black-middle-class norms, than he ever admitted); and then his lifelong curiosity led the young Wright to wonder what the curtains would look like if he set them on fire. The result was a house in flames; and, since fire is one of the most persistent images in much of his work, this incident may be the source. Terrified, he hid *under* the house. At four, he was an underground man; and he thereby incarnated a motif which appears throughout his work. For his deed, his mother lashed him so hard he lost consciousness.

From Natchez the Wrights moved in 1914 to Memphis, where the young Wright first experienced the disparity between a man-made and a natural environment: "In Memphis we lived in a one-story brick tenement. The stone buildings and the concrete pavements looked bleak and hostile to me. The absence of green, growing things made the city seem dead."[3] Because his family was poor, he had to face all the attendant evils of poverty—worn-out clothing, substandard shelter, inadequate food. But his family was not only poor, it also ceased to be much of a family in the conventional sense; for, once in Memphis, Nathan Wright abandoned his family. As small children, Richard and his younger brother Leon, who was born in 1910, often had the "miss-meal-cramps" because they were so hungry. It seemed to Richard that he never had enough to eat; and, until well along in life, he was in fact thin and undernourished. Unfortunately for the memory of his father, Richard linked his empty stomach to the parent who had just left Mrs. Wright for another woman: "As the days slid past the image of my father became associated with my pangs of hunger, and whenever I felt hunger I thought of him with deep biological bitterness'' (22). Childishly ignorant of the structure of American society and its consequent pressures, the young Wright was perhaps overly harsh in his judgment of his father's rejection of his family. But the father's abandonment did, of course, result in a matrifocal unit in which the importance of men in Richard's early life was diminished and the influence of his mother and maternal grandmother was maximized.

And a broken family also made a hard young life even harder. Because Mrs. Wright now had to support her children with menial jobs, she often had to allow Richard and his brother to take care of themselves, frequently with expectedly sad results. In *Black Boy,* Wright's autobiography, he recounts how, when he was only six, saloon customers, plying him with alcohol to amuse themselves, taught the reeling child to say filthy words for pennies and made him a drunkard.

Stunned by his father's desertion of the family, Richard worried that his mother had also left him when she had to place both her children in an orphanage because she could not support them. After six weeks, she took her sons from the orphanage and moved with them to Elaine, Arkansas, where her sister and her husband lived. This early constant movement helps to explain Wright's ''outsiderness''—he moved so frequently as a child that he never felt the security created by living in the same place for a long time—and this pattern that was sustained throughout his life is reflected in his writing.

On the way to Elaine, they stopped for a while in Jackson, Mississippi, to visit with Mrs. Wright's parents, the Wilsons. There, when a schoolteacher who boarded in Mrs. Wilson's house told Wright the story of Bluebeard and his seven wives, ''the tale made the world around me be, throb, live'' (47). It was through language that the world took on more meaning than despotic fact would allow. Adumbrating her later power over her grandson, Granny interrupted the telling of the story by stepping onto her porch and ordering the schoolteacher to stop.

Their stay in Elaine began as a relatively pleasant idyll in the home of Aunt Maggie and her husband, Uncle Hoskins, where Richard finally got as much to eat as he needed; but the pleasure was soon to give way to nightmare for the youth. Wright says, ''I had no suspicion that I was to live here but a short time and that the manner of my leaving would be my first baptism of racial emotion" (58). Like the poets that Jean Wagner examines in *Black Poets of the United States*, Wright racializes religion in such a way that race and religion become symbolically intertwined; and this intermingling occurs in a writer who repeatedly and stridently declared his secularism. The "racial baptism" was the murder of Uncle Hoskins by whites who coveted his lucrative saloon and the subsequent flight of his widow and the Wright family to West Helena, near Elaine.

After his mother was partially paralyzed by a stroke, Granny took her and the boys back to Jackson, Mississippi, where life was still almost too hard for Richard. Mrs. Wright's condition regressed to the point that "once in the night, my mother called me to her bed and told me that she could not endure the pain, that she wanted to die. I held her hand and begged her to be quiet. That night I ceased to react to my mother. . . . At the age of twelve . . . I had . . . a conviction that the meaning of living came only when one was struggling to wring a meaning out of meaningless suffering" (111-12). Wright never recovered from the painfulness of his youth in the misery of the Deep South; it is the central, defining event of his existence, like the death of Arthur Henry Hallam in Tennyson's life or the elopement with Elizabeth Barrett in Robert Browning's. As such, this painful experience is the source of much, if not most, of Wright's best work.

The financial burden on Granny of keeping both Richard's mother and the two boys was eventually too great, forcing the family to send Leon to Aunt Maggie, who had moved to Detroit, and Richard to Greenwood, Mississippi, to live with his Uncle Clark and Aunt Jody. At Uncle Clark's, Wright recalls that he was whipped for swearing and commanded by Uncle Clark to reveal where he had learned such language. Wright muses in his autobiography, "How could I have told him that I had learned to curse before I had learned to read? How could I have told him that I had been a drunkard at the age of six?" (109). The continual strain of self-pity in Wright's account of his early life is perhaps unavoidable, but it flaws his autobiography: the reader feels sorry for Wright without his insisting upon it.

In the early 1920s the adolescent Wright returned to Jackson, and from 1921 to 1925 he received a large portion of the only formal education he ever got—first at the Jim Hill Public School and then at the Smith-Robinson Public School, from which he was graduated as valedictorian. His formal education was not lavish and, as such, was surely a stumbling block to a man of letters, but it was not so sparse as Wright indicates in *Black Boy* in order to make more impressive his credentials as a proletarian prodigy: he surely had more education than most Deep-South blacks in the 1920s. Nor was he as unhappy as a youth as he would have one imagine.[4]

One cause of contentment for Wright in that wretched environment was reading, which, along with writing, saved him from the brutalization and degradation that were so frequent in the rural South among blacks and whites. He reports that even as a small child "I told my mother that I wanted to learn to read and she encouraged me. Soon I was able to pick my way through most of the children's books I ran across. There grew in me a consuming curiosity about what was happening around me" (29). Because he read, he learned not just from experience but also from other people's imaginations—especially, in his youth, from Horatio Alger's. Perhaps it is because his mind was kept busy with the written word that he was able to neglect to learn the bit of intelligence that the South most wanted to pass along to him—his inferiority: he never forgot he was human, despite the fact that the denial of his personhood was the primary objective of white indoctrination.

It was also in these truncated school years that he had the pleasure of becoming a published writer. His brief story entitled "The Voodoo of Hell's Half Acre" appeared in 1924 in the *Southern Register*, a black newspaper published in Jackson. Unfortunately, no copy of the story is available, though the typesetter for the paper related her memory of how it began to Michel Fabre, the author of *The Unfinished Quest of Richard Wright*. The story, she says, begins with the narrator's memories of sixth-grade mischiefs that he made with a friend, who is interestingly named Bigger Thomas (*Quest*, p. 48). The experience of publishing a story confirmed Wright's suspicion that he was an exception to the rule of environmental determinism—because, for every Richard Wright that Mississippi produced, there were thousands of products like his father; and, to Wright, "I was building up in me a dream which the entire educational system of the South had been rigged to stifle" (186).

One of the greatest immediate causes for his sensation of stiflement was his life with his grandmother. Wright loathed her fanatical Seventh-Day Adventism, which left him with a permanently secular imagination and an adamant, uncompromising hostility toward religious solutions to earthly problems. Although the reader may sympathize with him in his rejection of Granny's religion, with its repression and bleakness, it should be pointed out that his loathing of it had the serious consequence of preventing him from seeing the church's vital sociological function in the black community. The black church is the only independent black institution in America and the traditional center of black culture; as such, it deserves credit that Wright studiously withheld from it. The church was the one place in the Deep South where blacks could release the pressures caused by white racism and was therefore necessary to emotional sanity. But Wright was so rebellious toward other-worldliness that he was blind to its secular utility, regardless of whether it was ultimately piffle or not. However, the black church and his grandmother's millennialism influenced Wright nonetheless: they gave him the themes and the imagery that, secularized, informed the writing that he did to maintain his emotional stability.

But it was the regulation of his life at his grandmother's house that infuriated the adolescent Wright more than did her religiosity—until he threatened to run away from home, she would not allow him to work on Saturday, the Adventist Sabbath. His Aunt Addie, who shared the house with them, was equally frustrating. When Addie tried to beat him at home for eating walnuts in school (he was innocent), he resisted by pulling a knife on her: violence was at the very center of his life, as well as of his work. Even in this teenage crisis, though, Wright's readers are assured that he behaved nobly: "Since I was alone with her, and desperate, I cast my loyalties aside and told her the name of the guilty boy, feeling that he merited no consideration" (119).

According to Wright, he was the only sensitive, high-minded boy in the black community; but it is amply clear that it was often sauciness and high spirits that ruled his behavior, not courtliness! In *Black Boy* he relates how, as a small child who was being bathed by Granny, he told her: "softly but unpremeditatedly" to

" 'kiss back there' " (49), his anus. The innocence he typically feigns here is not convincing; and the reader begins to resist his portrait of himself as always the sensitive and misunderstood child in a caustic environment. Since Wright knew beforehand all too well the meaning of his contemptuous words to Granny, he clearly caused that elderly woman as much irritation with his verbal ability as she ever caused him with her religion. Nor is his sarcasm appealing: "God blessed our home with the love that binds" (121).

He was finally successful enough in his revolt against Addie and Granny that he was allowed to look seriously for a job, which resulted in an opportunity for employment with a white family. The job interview, recorded in *Black Boy*, is notable for its bitter humor and for Wright's admirable handling of dialogue, one of the aspects of writing he does best:

> "Do you want this job?" the woman asked.
> "Yes, ma'am," I said, afraid to trust my own judgment.
> "Now, boy, I want to ask you one question and I want you to tell me the truth," she said.
> "Yes, ma'am," I said, all attention.
> "Do you steal?" she asked me seriously.
> I burst into a laugh, then checked myself.
> "What's so damn funny about that?" she asked.
> "Lady, if I was a thief, I'd never tell anybody."
> "What do you mean?" she blazed with a red face.
> I had made a mistake during my first five minutes in the white world. I hung my head.
> "No, ma'am," I mumbled, "I don't steal." (160)

The interview recalls Mr. Dalton's query in *Native Son* of Bigger Thomas about whether or not he steals. In both cases, of course, only a fool, which Mr. Dalton and the white woman assume their prospective employees are, would admit having committed a crime. But one wonders about Wright's ingenuousness: did he really forget to play the expected role, or is he scoring points, as he so frequently wants to do? More revealing than the job interview is the woman's indignation about his proclamation of wanting to become a writer: in scorning this ambition, she violates his selfhood, his manhood. This lack of respect for his plan to be a writer is also the basic reason he was uncomfortable in the Communist party: it tried to regulate his writing, which is another way of saying that it tried to tell him what he was, just as the Deep South had.

As he realized more and more the human and aesthetic sterility of Jackson and the South, he knew he had to leave, and he stole for a while in order to get enough money to flee to Memphis. He also worked for a time at a hotel, where he bootlegged liquor. According to Ralph Ellison, the incident at the hotel involving a white prostitute and her customer that Wright relates in his autobiography is not factually true;[5] for Wright had borrowed the story from an incident Ellison had told him about his own life and had applied it to himself:

> A huge, snowy-skinned blonde took a room on my floor. One night she rang for service and I went to wait upon her. She was in bed with a thickset man; both were nude and uncovered. She said that she wanted some liquor, and slid out of bed and waddled across the floor to get her money from the dresser drawer. Without realizing it, I watched her.
>
> "Nigger, what in hell are you looking at?" the white man asked, raising himself upon his elbows.
>
> "Nothing, sir," I answered, looking suddenly miles deep into the blank walls of the room.
>
> "Keep your eyes where they belong if you want to be healthy!"
>
> "Yes, sir." (221-22)

As this example indicates, Wright sacrifices historical fact on the altar of imaginative and emotional truth in his autobiography. The same basic scene, with alterations, appears in *The Long Dream*.

He "arrived in Memphis on a cold November Sunday morning, in 1925" (228), and, by means of several different jobs, he was able to save enough money to bring his mother and brother to join him. In one of the jobs, at an optical company, he relates that he delivered a pair of glasses and met a "tall, florid-faced white man" who "was unmistakably a Yankee, for his physical build differed sharply from that of the lanky Southerner" (252). For one bedeviled all of his life by the existence of prejudice in the world, Wright's own uncritical acceptance of stereotypical notions is embarrassing—but, as his statement indicates, even a writer of Wright's acute perception is not immune to such nonsense. Another incident in his optical company saga deserves mention:

some whites were able to engage him in a boxing match with Harrison, a young black who worked for a rival optical firm. Not only does this incident presage the Battle Royal in Ralph Ellison's *Invisible Man*, but it also dramatizes the way whites have been able to get blacks to fight each other rather than the real enemy.

But Wright's two-year stopover in Memphis on his way to the Promised Land of the North is chiefly important not for the menial jobs he took but for the reading he did. When he was able through subterfuge to borrow H. L. Mencken's *A Book of Prefaces* and *Prejudices* from the library, he was profoundly impressed by Mencken's vision of the South as hell: Wright had not known that his own perceptions were not unique. Not only were there people who felt as he did, but they made their feelings known. Wright was also astounded to see that Mencken "was fighting, fighting with words. He was using words as a weapon, using them them as one would use a club. Could words be weapons?" (272). From infancy Wright had sensed that language had overwhelming power. After his father told young Richard to kill a kitten that would not stop meowing, Wright purposely took his words literally in order to gain a victory over a force more powerful than himself; he actually killed the poor cat. Wright's unvarying, instinctive, and lifelong response to his questioning whether words have power was an overwhelmingly affirmative reply.

Finally, he was able to flee Memphis and go North. By the time he was only nineteen, he had left the plantation for the ghetto, the feudal period for the modern, and the agricultural society for the industrial. Later, a permanent outsider, he would leave Chicago for New York, New York for Paris, and Paris for various parts of the world. Freedom of movement, geographical and intellectual, was one of Wright's deepest concerns; but his revolt from the village was quintessentially American and took him less far than he had imagined—for, like James Joyce, who left Ireland but wrote about nothing else, Wright took the Deep South with him however far he traveled. Since he never recovered from the experience of being black in the white South, his literary imagination was permanently structured by the South's refusal to acknowledge the humanity of black people. And so, paradoxically, although Richard Wright speaks with often violent repudiation of American society, his work is also a testimony to its power. Wright, like Malcolm X, is in the characteristically American, Horatio Alger tradition; for, to both writers, one can achieve an individual apocalypse through thrift and hard work.

The decade in Chicago was almost as crucial to Wright's development as his nineteen years in the South were. The destruction of black folk values that has been delineated so powerfully by William Attaway in *Blood on the Forge* (1941) was observed by Wright in Chicago and rendered in his own writing. Not the Promised Land, the South Side black ghetto of Chicago that Wright learned to know so intimately was an inferno for black emigrants from the South who, like Wright himself, reached Chicago as provincials. As usual, he had to support himself with menial jobs: the first one was as a delivery boy for a Jewish delicatessen; his next, as a dishwasher for a cafeteria; in the summer of 1928, as a worker in the post office; the latter job gave him impressions he was able to use in *Lawd Today* and *The Outsider*. His experiences left him with no illusions about the joys of proletarian labor. "By this time [1928] he was seriously contemplating a literary career" (*Quest*, 79). After the Great Depression eliminated his job at the post office, he accepted a position with an insurance company that cheated its black clients; but, during his tenure as an insurance agent, he fueled his literary imagination as he visited many black homes in which he observed the effects of urbanization on people whose grandparents had been slaves on southern plantations.

When Wright eventually lost this job, he went on relief in 1931; but he continued his writing and his devouring of many novelists—Dostoevsky, Tolstoy, Stephen Crane, Joseph Conrad, Theodore Dreiser, John Dos Passos. In this same year he began work on *Lawd Today*, which was published posthumously in 1963; but he wrote and published his short story "Superstition" in *Abbott's Monthly Magazine*[6] only because he was under severe financial pressures which had been brought about by the arrival of his mother and brother, who were both in frail health and unable to work. This story, advertising its debt to Edgar Allan Poe in its Gothic atmosphere and theme, also glances at a concern that was later central to Wright's literary landscape: the emptiness of human existence. After the second of two deaths in the story, both of which occur at a family reunion, Wright's narrator says, "It [the moment of the second death] displayed the very worthlessness and nothingness of what they called life. It was amazing by its very blackness!" (73). The young author disowned "Superstition" by never again using his middle name when signing a publication (he had signed it "Richard Nathanael Wright"). Ironically, he was never paid for the piece.

In 1933 Wright took a job as an orderly in the Michael Reese Hospital, an experience he recounted in "The Man Who Went to Chicago" (1945) and in "What You Don't Know Won't Hurt You" (1942). After he lost his job at the hospital, he took another one as a supervisor in the South Side Boys' Club in Chicago's black ghetto. He learned more about the Bigger Thomases of America, because he could see in an urban context in the boys' club his own frustrations in Mississippi. For a while he worked on the Illinois Federal Writers' Project, a branch of the Works Project Administration. Then came his membership in 1932 in the John Reed Club, which, with Communist support, was supposed to use art for revolutionary ends. Although Marxism gave Wright a permanent orientation, sympathy, and mode of analysis, it also effected a confusion in his writing which was never resolved: the conflict between race and class. In 1932, however, what was important to him about the John Reed Club was that it gave him what he felt he had never had before: continuous support and understanding. He became so important to the club that he was elected secretary without even running for the position. He helped organize a lecture series for the club and delivered a lecture himself on black revolutionary poetry to the Indianapolis John Reed Club. When he joined the Communist party, possibly at the end of 1933, he made one of the few strong pledges in his life; for, though he was later severely disillusioned by the party's Stalinist tactics, it was extremely important at the time in his intellectual development.

I *Political Poetry*

The year 1933 was a watershed for Wright, "since he began his literary career as a revolutionary poet" (*Quest*, 95). After he joined the John Reed Club, he began writing his revolutionary poems ("I Have Seen Black Hands," "We of the Streets," "Red Leaves of Red Books," for example) for such leftist journals as *Left Front*, *New Masses*, *International Literature*, and *New Challenge*. With one exception, the poems are negligible as literature; they tend to be crude Marxist propaganda. Typical of them is Wright's "I Have Seen Black Hands," published in 1934 in *New Masses*, which is essentially a Whitmanesque cataloguing of black hands working, praying, and grasping for freedom. The poem concludes apocalyptically with the promise that white and black hands will be raised together in the Marxist workers' millennium:

III

I am black and I have seen black hands, millions and millions of them—
Reaching hesitantly out of days of slow death for the goods they had
  made, but the bosses warned that the goods were private and
  did not belong to them,
And the black hands struck desperately out in defence of life and there
  was blood, but the enraged bosses decreed that this too was wrong,
And the black hands felt the cold steel bars of the prison they had made,
  in despair tested their strength and found that they could neither
  bend nor break them,
And the black hands lifted palms in mute and futile supplication to the
  sodden faces of mobs wild in the revelries of sadism,
And the black hands strained and clawed and struggled in vain at the
  noose that tightened about the black throat,
And the black hands waved and beat fearfully at the tall flames that
  cooked and charred the black flesh. . . .

IV

I am black and have seen black hands
Raised in fists of revolt, side by side with the white fists of white
  workers,
And some day—and it is only this which sustains me—
Some day there shall be millions and millions of them,
One red day in a burst of fists on a new horizon![7]

Much of the poetry Wright published in the 1930s is a deification of the proletariat from a self-consciously Marxist perspective. For example, "Spread Your Sunrise," which was published in *New Masses*, is a crude exhortation to a child of the Revolution to paint the world red. The more impressive "We of the Streets," which was published in April 1937, is a celebration of the urban masses who are forced to live their lives on America's streets. Wright dramatically imagines the narrator as an anonymous member of the group in this free-verse, lyrical hymn of praise, which nonetheless includes his characteristic harsh realism: "Our strip of sky is a dirty shirt."[8]

His central poetic strategy in "We of the Streets" is the urbanization of nature: the sea has become "water swirling in gutters"; lightning, "the blue flame of an acetylene torch"; a flower, the color of a billboard; thunder, the roar of the "L" train. Such transmogrification is the lot of millions of black folk who have been wrenched by hunger and privation from their agrarian South into concrete ghettoes where, no richer than before, they are even deprived of their beloved green earth. Yet these amazing, enduring emigrants from nature humanize even the hell of industrialization:

> Our emblems are street emblems: stringy curtains blowing in windows; sticky-fingered babies tumbling on door-steps; deep-cellared laughs meant for everybody; slow groans heard in area-ways.
> Our sunshine is a common hope; our common summer and common winter a common joy and a common sorrow; our fraternity the shoulder-rubbing crude with unspoken love; our password the wry smile that speaks a common fate.
> Our love is nurtured by the soft flares of gas-lights; our hate is an icy wind screaming around corners.

But, expectedly, these remarkable people who have managed to nurture lovingly their young in squalid brick and mortar nests are left by their efforts "worn hard like pavement"; and these folk who, ghettoized, lead so much of their lives in common, will someday protest their oppression collectively. The poem is basically an appreciation, not a battle cry or an exhortation to man the barricades, but its conclusion, though vague and remote in tone, implicitly but unmistakably promises change: "And there is something in the streets that made us feel immortality when we rushed along ten thousand strong, hearing our chant fill the world, wanting to do what none of us would do alone, aching to shout the forbidden word, knowing that we of the streets are deathless. . . ."

"We of the Streets," particularly in its ending, which stresses organized proletarian revolt, suggests the tension the young Marxist Wright experienced in deciding between being a class spokesman and an individual. His insistent ego eventually and finally made him more comfortable speaking for himself than either for a class or a race, but this particular poetic effort to quiet his individuality is rather successful.

Though "We of the Streets" is one of Wright's better poems, it is also characteristic of his poetic corpus in that it is typically loose in syntax and organization; its only organizing principle seems to be a listing or cataloguing. His poetry, which is usually prose set into stanzas, dispenses with many devices associated with verse in favor of a Socialist Realism that is sincere but unrefined.

Such, too, is the case with "Hearst Headline Blues," in which Wright advertises his debt to John Dos Passos by comprising the poem entirely of newspaper headlines (they are also a device of which he later made prominent use in *Native Son*). The use of headlines tightens the poem's syntax and gives it a laconic quality that is absent from much of Wright's proletarian verse—a terse quality that reappears at the end of his career in his *haiku* poems. The headlines Wright chooses evoke the social and political ambience of the 1930s—depression, communism, racism—and strong social reference is one of his most characteristic traits. The kaleidoscopic series of headlines that comprise the poem also suggests the sensationalism associated with the Hearst newspapers of the 1930s: "Weeps When He Learns He Married His Sister,"[9] "Professor Simpson Lectures on Sperm," "Broker Rapes and Murders Maid," "Starvation Claims Mother and Tot," "Father Butchers Son with Axe." The poem is notable for the writer's attempt to create a blues lyric out of such sensational journalistic captions.

Wright's "Red Leaves of Red Books," published in *New Masses* on April 30, 1935, is simply repetition of the command to the pages of Marxist literature to "turn" until "the calloused hands that grip you/Are hardened to the steel of unretractable purpose!"[10] The Communist pages are to turn in white and black hands, in the hands of men and women, young and old, in every part of America. Fortunately, the poem is short. Like most of Wright's Depression-era poetry, these verses are too weak to carry the weight of Marxist tract:

Turn
Red leaves of red books
Turn
In white palms and black palms
Turn
Slowly in the mute hours of the night
Turn
In the fingers of women and the fingers of men
In the fingers of the old and the fingers of the young.

The one unquestionable exception to the generalization that Wright's poetry is pedestrian is "Between the World and Me," which was first printed in *Partisan Review* in 1935, and which has since then been reprinted. The narrator, initially unidentified, stumbles across "the thing"[11] in the woods; this "thing," the reader later learns, is the remains of a black man after a lynching. "The sooty details of the scene rose, thrusting themselves between the world and me. . . ." "A vacant shoe, an empty tie, a ripped shirt, a lonely hat, and a pair of trousers stiff with black blood." The lynch mob has literally denied the black man his manhood by castrating him, although the depicted carnival atmosphere of the poem suggests frivolity—"upon the trampled grass were buttons, dead matches, butt-ends of cigars and cigarettes, peanut shells, a drained gin-flask, and a whore's lipstick." The narrator then discovers that the victim has been tarred and feathered, and finally burned. In a leap of the imagination, the speaker becomes the lynched man:

The sun died in the sky; a night wind muttered in the grass and fumbled the leaves in the trees; the woods poured forth the hungry yelping of hounds; the darkness screamed with thirsty voices; and the witnesses rose and lived:
The dry bones stirred, rattled, lifted, melting themselves into my bones.
The grey ashes formed flesh firm and black, entering into my flesh.

By switching the point of view from onlooker to participant, Wright gives the reader an internal as well as an external report of a lynching. "And the down and quills of the white feathers sank into my raw flesh, and I moaned in my agony./Then my blood was cooled mercifully, cooled by a baptism of gasoline." Wright typically mocks the moral pretensions of a Christian community by using the word "baptism." At the end of this very powerful poem, the original speaker is "the thing." To Wright, who grew up amidst stories of the lynching, the castration, and the tarring and feathering of black men, lynching, symbolic to him of his race's status in America, was the South's ultimate weapon in its battle to keep him and his fellow blacks in their place.

II *Grapplings with Communism and Artistic Growth*

Wright was not too long a member of the Communist party before he learned that writing and political activity do not always combine easily. As he later described in "I Tried to Be a Communist," the autobiographical sketch that deals with his experiences in and disillusionments with the party, he was led into the John Reed Club (an organization for Communist artists and writers) by the idea "that here at last, in a realm of revolutionary expression, Negro experiences could find a home, a functioning value and role."[12] He was breathless at the prospect of getting published in widely read Communist periodicals, rapt by club members' promises to help him with his writing in order that he might become a more eloquent lure to potential black Communists.

But Wright quickly learned that venal, costly party demands for such trivia as posterboard for sloganeering all too often preempted literary fundings; and he was eventually dazed to hear plans for increasing recruitment monies by shutting down altogether the John Reed Club's literary magazine, *Left Front*, despite the fact that it was the chief drawing card to young literati. He noted grimly that as party emphasis shifted away from literature he was allowed to use less and less time and energy for writing and forced to spend an ever-increasing amount of time on party activities—he wanted to produce his literature, but the party wanted him to organize the South Side of Chicago. He soon felt that the Communists even wanted control over his very mental cast: the party was firm in its wish that conflicts be accounted for solely on Marxist grounds and ignored the ethnicity that Wright perceived to play such a large role in social problems; it had opinions about what materials would be "suitable" imaginative grist for Wright's imagination; and it even dared to suggest to him what literary strategies he might choose.

Though by 1934 Wright was chafing mightily at the Communist party, it was not until the John Reed Club called a national conference in that year that he become overtly and publicly angry with communism. Though he had greeted the conference with enthusiasm, naively hoping that it would deal with writing problems, his mood blackened when its convening move was to make official the termination of *Left Front*. Since Wright perceived little point to a literary organization that had no journal for publication, and because he felt that literary people should not band together under the aegis of a club that purported to encourage writing but in fact made its members march endlessly in picket lines, he called glumly for a dissolution of the clubs. His suggestion was greeted by howls from all sides that he was a "defeatist": although members privately agreed with him, they would not defend him publicly.

Thus it was surely with an "Alice in Wonderland" sense of unreality that Wright heard only shortly after his public upbraiding that an official decision had been made to close the clubs and replace them with new "People's Front" organizations. It was this announcement of intent to close the John Reed Clubs that enlightened Wright as to the truly cynical nature of the Communist party:

> I asked what was to become of the young writers whom the Communist Party had implored to join the clubs and who were ineligible for this new group, and there was no answer. "This thing is Cold!" I exclaimed to myself. To effect a swift change in policy, the Communist Party was dumping one organization, then organizing a new scheme with entirely new people.
>
> I found myself arguing alone against majority opinion and then I made still another amazing discovery. I learned that when a man was informed of the wish of the party he submitted, even though he knew with all the strength of his brain that the wish was not a wise one. . . . I had spent a third of my life traveling from the place of my birth to the North just to talk freely, to escape the pressure of fear. And now I was facing fear again.[13]

The 1934 conference closed with the resolution to reconvene in the summer of 1935 as the first American Writers' Congress.

Wright's contribution to that second convention was a lonely dissension to the congress's formal resolution to abolish the John Reed Clubs—once again Wright's fellow Communists were of like mind about his position but dared not to voice it. But Wright felt less wounded this second time he was publicly deserted by those who agreed with him, for he had become emotionally estranged from the Communist party and was even indifferent to the activities of the Writers' Congress.

Wright's next two years, his last in Chicago, were characterized not only by intense irritation with the Communist party, but by literary ferment. The only real benefit that Wright had accrued from attending the disappointing Writers' Congress was his introduction to James T. Farrell, which signaled "the beginning of a literary friendship that benefited Wright enormously" (*Quest*, 119), particularly since Wright's attention was turning toward the short story. And though 1935, the year of the Writers' Congress, heralded for Wright the rejection of "Cesspool" (later *Lawd Today*) by both Knopf and Scribner's, it also saw the writing of what may well be Wright's most brilliant short story, "Big Boy Leaves Home." While working for the Federal Project in this same year, he also directed his literary energies toward research on the history of Illinois and of blacks in Chicago.

In February 1936 he helped with the National Negro Congress; by April, he was more or less the head of the South Side Writers' Group (which included Fenton Johnson, Frank Marshall Davis, and Margaret Walker): it was to this group that, toward the end of 1936, Wright read a version of "Bright and Morning Star." When "Big Boy Leaves Home" was accepted in that same year for publication in an anthology called *The New Caravan*, "he was for the first time being noticed by the non-Communist white press" (*Quest*, 133), for this short story was recognized as the best piece in the anthology by reviewers for the *New York Times*, *Saturday Review of Literature*, and the *New Republic*. Thus, with the success of "Big Boy Leaves Home," Wright's ties to his Chicago Communist cell weakened still further, because his grievances against the party could no longer be tempered merely by his pleasure in seeing his revolutionary poetry published in *New Masses*.

Yet he was not ready to quit the party wholly and officially, only to sever his ties with the Chicago branch, which he felt had intentionally and unfairly hampered his artistry. He quarreled with the Chicago party leaders and found a more suitable niche for himself in New York as Harlem editor for the *Daily Worker*; but he was able to take this job only because the New York Communists were unaware of his split with the Chicago branch. Wright was happy to go to New York because the publishers were there and he believed that he would have a better chance of being published if he represented himself instead of relying on an agent. So, after having spent a decade in Chicago, he began another one in New York, beginning in 1937.

During the summer and fall of that year, he wrote over two hundred articles for the *Worker*; and the same year marked the publication of "Blueprint for Negro Writing" in *New Challenge*. "This essay is the most complete, coherent, and profound statement of Wright's theories on Afro-American writing" (*Quest*, 151). Essentially, what Wright attempts to do in this essay is to argue that black American literature is of necessity racially nationalistic since blacks have been excluded from white American culture, and that this black nationalism should be viewed from a Marxist perspective. This conflation of racial ethos and Marxism causes repeated confusion in Wright's work because each seemed to him to have certain claims of primacy over the other—and he vacillated between the two.

He also touches on another of his central concerns in this essay—the notion that, since blacks left a premodern way of life for the modern world in a very brief time span, they suffered mental dislocation. The year 1937 was also a landmark for him because he met and talked often with Ralph Ellison and because he won with his narrative "Fire and Cloud" the first prize of $500 in a contest sponsored by *Story* magazine. He now found it easier to get major publishing houses to print his work; and, when his first published book, *Uncle Tom's Children*, appeared in 1938, it made him "one of the literary stars of the Party" (*Quest*, 162).

During this literary rise of 1937-38 he was living with the Sawyers, a kind but nearly illiterate mother and daughter who accepted him as part of the family and who helped him stretch his small funds. "Unfortunately, Wright let himself become romantically involved with the young daughter [Marion] of the house and only barely escaped marrying her . . ." (*Quest*, 169). After Mrs.

Sawyer had announced the daughter's impending marriage to Wright on May 22, 1938, Wright learned that she had syphilis, although of a congenital, noncommunicable variety; he broke off with her permanently and, of course, lost the Sawyers' hospitality. After his romance with shy, reserved Marion Sawyer, he had brief attachments to two other women: one was a member of the bourgeoisie so disliked by Communist Wright; the other, a beautiful, brainless, married woman. "There is no doubt that Wright's hesitations were caused by his attraction to the many different attributes which he hoped to find in one woman, and with time, he turned more and more toward white women" (*Quest*, 197).

Most of this year, 1938, was spent working on *Native Son* while Wright was living with a white family, the Newtons. In the meantime, *Uncle Tom's Children* was selling moderately well; and, after he had sent the typescript of *Native Son* to his editor at Harper's, Edward Aswell, in June 1939, the Book-of-the-Month Club made the novel its March 1940 selection. Early reviews were very favorable; the novel "sold 200,000 copies in under three weeks, breaking a twenty-year record at Harper's" (*Quest*, 180), and Wright was now famous. The Communist critics, because of the novel's mixture of Marxism and black pride, were not completely comfortable with the book, but they restrained their criticisms because they wanted Wright's prestige in the war against capitalism. Although he spent part of 1939 working on a novel entitled "Little Sister," a narrative that has black and white characters, this work has not been published.

In 1939, the year in which he won a Guggenheim Fellowship, he met two white women who, he thought, fufilled his demands for a wife: Ellen Poplar and Dhimah Rose Meadman. Although he felt great physical attraction for Dhimah, he apparently married her because he felt that Ellen would reject a proposal from him. In July or August 1939, to Ellen's dismay, he married Dhimah, but their honeymoon was postponed to March 1940, when they went to Mexico. Because Wright discovered how little he and Dhimah had in common, they returned home separately and never reconciled. Dhimah went directly to New York, but her husband returned by way of the South in order to see Mississippi and his relatives again. After his divorce from Dhimah, Wright married Ellen Poplar on March 12, 1941. Their first daughter, Julia, was born April 15, 1942.

During July 1940 he and Paul Green collaborated in Chapel Hill on the dramatic version of *Native Son*, and the play opened on Broadway in 1941 under the direction of Orson Welles. Except for the Hearst-controlled newspapers (William Randolph Hearst hated Welles because of *Citizen Kane*, a film Welles directed, which was inspired by the life of Hearst), the press reacted favorably to the play. When Wright had agreed to collaborate with Paul Green on the stage adaptation of *Native Son*, he had also consented to write the text for a folk history of Afro-Americans that was to contain photographs by Edwin Rosskam. When the book was published in October 1941 it received enthusiastic reviews. While finishing this book, *Twelve Million Black Voices*, Wright was also writing two novels—"Black Hope" (unpublished) and "The Man Who Lived Underground," which had only its third section published as a short story in 1944; and he was working, too, on his still unpublished screenplay, "Melody Limited," based on the history of the Jubilee Singers of Fisk.

The April 1943 visit to Fisk University that prompted Wright's screenplay also caused him to think about his past; and as a result he wrote his autobiography during 1943-44. "On December 17, 1943, he sent Reynolds [his agent] the manuscript, which covered his life up to his departure from Chicago in 1937" (*Quest*, 253). This work, called "American Hunger," is not to be confused with *American Hunger* (1977), which is the second section of the original manuscript. The first section was published as *Black Boy*; the *Atlantic Monthly* accepted for publication the part that was about Wright's stormy membership in, and eventual repudiation of, the Communist party, and that was entitled "I Tried to Be a Communist" (1944).[14] The publication of that article signaled Wright's formal break with the Communists, though the piece puts May Day 1936 as his moment of departure. However, that date seems an odd one to denote Wright's official exit because he continued to edit the *Daily Worker* for two years after that! His asserted date of quitting the party may well be one of the declarations that caused some critics to level the charges of revisionism of personal history against the *Atlantic* publication. One of his biographers has noted of the piece that "it is to be read with caution: it suffers from some reversals in the chronological sequence of events as well as significant omissions" (*Quest*, p. 540, n. 1).

III *Mid-life Self-assessments*

Mid-life is traditionally a period of stocktaking, a time when offspring finally struggle to come to an accurate assessment of their parents and of their half-finished lives; and Wright was no exception. During the mid 1940s, "his personal life was serene. . . . Ellen had become the essential element of his stability, and he left more and more of the practical responsibility of their life to her" (*Quest*, 275). Wright, now in his early to mid-thirties, finally had in his private life an atmosphere ideally suited to psychological reflection.

He took great advantage of the soothing lull by setting himself to the task of describing his youthful life and in making rational sense of the southern black culture from which he came. His previous masterpiece, *Native Son*, was extraordinarily insightful and consistent in its racial assertions but was not the emotional catharsis that Wright now demanded—*Native Son* was a record of *urban* black experience and therefore less emotionally charged for Wright than the southern hell of his formative years, and it was about a visceral beast, not a complex, brilliant human being, Richard Wright. Wright's next major works, *Twelve Million Black Voices: A Folk History of the Negro in the United States* (1941) and *Black Boy, A Record of Childhood and Youth* (1945), while largely internally consistent, are wildly divergent one from the other in their discussion of the black southern experience, with which both deal. Much has been made of Wright's feelings, positive and negative, of racial pride; but the discussions have not been based on *both* books. It has not been understood that Wright, in facing squarely the divergent tugs all humans must feel, reaches a sane and balanced assessment of his racial feelings in the two books when they are taken together as a unity.

In a sense *Twelve Million Black Voices* is as much an autobiography as *Black Boy*: it is a baring of his essence, which is his southern black folk origins. For all those who, like Margaret Walker or Cecil M. Brown, aver that Wright lacks racial pride, either because of his racial frankness in *Native Son* or because of his subsequent tirade in *Black Boy* against black ways that by all rights should have dragged him down, it is important to underscore the following passage, which is central to *Twelve Million*

Black Voices: "A child is a glad thing in the black stretches of the cotton country, and our gold is in the hearts of the people we love, in the veins that carry our blood, upon those faces where we catch furtive glimpses of the shape of our humble souls."[15] Such a poetical statement of love, which could easily have come from Jean Toomer's celebrated *Cane* or Wright's own "I Have Seen Black Hands," can only reflect deep racial pride. The book, photo-directed by Edwin Rosskam, is a brief, lyrical, imaginative recounting of the souls of the black *folk*, and not of W. E. B. DuBois's "talented tenth," a luminous example of which is treated in *Black Boy*. More eloquent sometimes than the text in the celebration of black folk ways are Rosskam's photographs, which depict a people brutalized beyond belief, yet still intact, still vital.

Behind Wright's commentary lies the already-noted thesis of so much of his work: in moving from a rural, agrarian, preindividualist culture to an urban, industrial, individualist one, blacks have undergone in a few hundred years what whites went through over several thousands of years; and blacks must feel pride that they have done as well as they have in the face of those upheavals. While comparison with a standard survey of Afro-American history like *From Plantation to Ghetto*, by August Meier and Elliott Rudwick, reveals some factual errors, Wright's essential, poetical truth remained inviolate for the mass of black people in 1941. Of course, Wright was not and never claimed to be an innovator either in history or in sociological theory, and his acknowledgment in the preface of his reliance on E. Franklin Frazier, Louis Wirth, and Horace R. Cayton indicates this fact.

The book is organized historically. Part One, "Our Strange Birth," covers the 250 years from 1619 to the so-called Emancipation Proclamation. Himself a chafing victim of the matrifocal tendencies inherent within the black family, Wright transcends his hostility and explains sadly the phenomenon in terms of the Middle Passage: "The slave ships . . . were floating brothels for the slave traders of the seventeenth and eighteenth centuries. Bound by heavy chains, we gazed impassively upon the lecherous crew members as they vented the pent-up bestiality of their starved sex lives upon our sisters and wives. This was a peculiar practice which, as the years flowed past, grew into a clandestine but well-established institution which the owners of cotton and tobacco plantations upheld, and which today, in large measure, accounts for the widespread mulatto population in the United States'' (14). The emotional emasculation of black men began before the slaves had reached the New World. Although there is much more to the alienation between black men and women than uncontested sexual violation, it nevertheless is crucial, as Wright realized.

Also notable is the persistence of a religious orientation in the antireligious Wright, who in *Black Boy* champs and rages at his grandmother's millennialism: ''When we were sick, we were thrown alive into the sea and the captain, pilgrim of progress, would studiously enter into the ship's log two words that would balance all *earthly* accounts—'jettisoned cargo' '' (15)—his implication being that divine sanctions obtain. Wright's commonest posture is of total self-reliance and this-worldliness—but, when he considers deeply the horrors of his life and his racial heritage, he often retreats, glancingly and instinctively, to the traditional solace that a belief in an afterlife brings; however, Wright always turns immediately back to passionless environmentalism.

He believes that, once on American soil, the black voyagers and their descendants became overwhelmingly influenced by the strange country to which they had been abducted; and in this conviction he aligns himself with sociologist E. Franklin Frazier, who strongly disagreed with Melville Herskovits's contention that remnants of African culture not only survive in America virtually unchanged after three centuries, but also continue to shape black reaction to experience. Herskovits further believes that these African cultural survivals, so steeped in tribal mystery to blacks as well as to whites, are, if ignored, a barrier to racial self-knowledge and to understanding between the races. Wright is as implacably opposed to the hint that American blacks' lives are shaped by inchoate remnants of tribal ways as he is to the thought that human progress might be guided by a divine hand—he finds much satisfaction in the notion that his race and he himself are the potential shapers of their own destinies.

Part Two, ''Inheritors of Slavery,'' includes the period from the Civil War until World War I. In a suggestive passage near the beginning, Wright emphasizes one of his favorite ideas—the presentness of the racial past: "Three hundred years are a long time for millions of folk like us to be held in such subjection, so long a time that perhaps scores of years will have to pass before we shall be able to express what this slavery has done to us, for our personalities are still numb from its long shocks; and, as the numbness leaves our souls, we shall yet have to feel and give utterance to the full pain we shall inherit" (31). Wright's prescience is evidenced by the fact that it was not until the Black Renaissance of the 1960s that Afro-American literature struck the note of authenticity which was almost never heard in the so-called Harlem Renaissance of the 1920s. The true themes of much black literature lie in the experience of slavery.

In the second part of *Twelve Million Black Voices* Wright also marshals together several miscellaneous points about language, racial relations, books, and the black church which he here recognizes as a central force in black history. Black English originated as a response to the pressure of slavery and as a result of the linguistic variety of the different tribes which were sources for slaves. In an implied acknowledgment that the fantastic ending of "Fire and Cloud," in which poor whites and blacks unite in the face of oppression, is merely wish-fulfillment, Wright remarks about the absurdity of poor whites and blacks fighting each other; but he also admits that this conflict is unfortunately the basic one in postbellum America. As for books, they, too, are cited as important in the post-Civil War period; for, "in a vague, sentimental sort of way we love books inordinately, even though we do not know how to read them, for we know that books are the gateway to a forbidden world" (64). In the egotistical *Black Boy*, too, Wright praises books as being a route out of misery but suggests most plainly that he stood virtually alone in taking advantage of them: it is manifest in *Twelve Million Black Voices* that he realizes that his black community was a strong force behind his embracing of books and an abiding one that will continue to push its questing youth toward literacy. His reliance on the redemptive power of reading puts him squarely within the tradition of black men such as Frederick Douglass and Malcolm X, who also praised the power of books in their autobiographies.

But in this section of Wright's work, it is a love for his race that informs the narration, as it is throughout the book:

For the most part our delicate families are held together by love, sympathy, pity, and the goading knowledge that we must work together to make a crop.

That is why we black folk laugh and sing when we are alone together. There is nothing—no ownership or lust for power—that stands between us and our kin. And we reckon kin not as others do, but down to the ninth and tenth cousin. And for a reason we cannot explain we are mighty proud when we meet a man, woman, or child who, in talking to us, reveals that the blood of our brood has somehow entered his being. Because our eyes are not blinded by the hunger for possessions, we are a tolerant folk. A black mother who stands in the sagging door of her gingerbread shack may weep as she sees her children straying off into the unknown world, but no matter what they may do, no matter what happens to them, no matter what crimes they may commit, no matter what the world may think of them, that mother always welcomes them back with an irreducibly human feeling that stands above the claim of law or property. (60-61)

This passage is too simple and tender in its claims for black motherhood and black community for its sincerity to be doubted. And, as such, it is surely the product of a great deal of Wright's mature reflection and earnest observation of his race since black motherly love was sometimes lacking in his own experience—his earliest memory is of hallucinating, after being beaten nearly to death by his mother for unintentionally setting a house-fire. Grotesque maternal images of "huge, wobbly white bags, like the full udders of cows"[16] crowded his reeling mind; and a lifelong ambivalence was born toward his mother, from whom he sought love and nurturance but too frequently received buffets. Wright did not even try to deny his varied feelings; his intelligence and integrity of vision made him simply accept that strong, loving motherhood is as much a truth and a mainstay of the black community as brutal beatings and emotional ambivalence were part of his life with his mother.

Part Three, which is concerned with the Great Migration and the resultant urbanization of rural southern blacks in northern ghettoes, includes a powerful statement about why the transition was so difficult:

Perhaps never in history has a more utterly unprepared folk wanted to go to the city; we were barely born as a folk when we headed for the tall and sprawling centers of steel and stone. We, who were landless upon the land; we, who had barely managed to live in family groups; we, who needed the ritual and guidance of institutions to hold our atomized lives together in lines of purpose; we, who had known only relationships to people and not relationships to things; we, who had never belonged to any organizations except the church and burial societies; we, who had had our personalities blasted away with two hundred years of slavery and had been turned loose to shift for ourselves—we were such a folk as this when we moved into a world that was destined to test all we were, that threw us into the scales of competition to weigh our mettle. And how were we to know that, the moment we landless millions of the land—we men who were struggling to be born—set our awkward feet upon the pavements of the city, life would begin to exact of us a heavy toll in death? (93)

Wright then emphasizes the appalling living conditions of the kitchenettes, where black families, like Bigger Thomas's, live in one room. "After working all day in one civilization, we go home to our Black Belts and live, within the orbit of the surviving remnants of the culture of the South, our naive, casual, verbal, fluid folk life" (127).

In the final section of *Twelve Million Black Voices*, which is entitled "Men in the Making," Wright makes it clear that "we black folk, our history and our present being, are a mirror to all the manifold experiences of America. What we want, what we represent, what we endure is what America is" (146). Quintessentially American, African Americans refuse to accept the prefabricated evaluation of themselves by Anglo-Saxon culture. They are becoming men; manhood, particularly in the broad sense of being able to choose what one is, is perhaps Wright's basic concern and is, for Wright, the essence of pride in one's self, one's race. *Twelve Million Black Voices* says about his people what *Black Boy* says about himself: its contentions are the fulcrums of his imaginative efforts.

Wright's biography of his people, published when he was in his early thirties, was emotionally rounded out and balanced by the fictionalized autobiography of himself as a youth, published four years later. These two works evidence that the two compelling aspects of reality for Wright were his blackness and his ego. Appropriately, when he deals with his Afro-Americanism, which is a collective phenomenon, in *Twelve Million Black Voices*, he uses the first-person plural "we" as his narrative voice. But when it is his extraordinary, utterly individualistic *ego* that he turns his attention to, it is a booming *I* that narrates *Black Boy*. Having sung out in pride for his race, he finds it necessary to repudiate black culture in *Black Boy* because of his ego—not only because he is so proud of his achievements that he must divorce them from his background so that he will have no one to thank for them but himself, but also because that ego which is *Black Boy*'s focus was genuinely threatened by some aspects of black culture. Although Wright's personal revolt against societal repressiveness was acted out as a child, he analyzed those strictures and his revulsion to them only as an adult. As a result, Wright by middle age sees himself as part of a noble racial ethos, a product of three centuries of legal and illegal slavery; but he is also an individualist who had to claw and scrabble and fight every moment of his early life to avoid being smothered by his culture. This ambivalence—integral, yet apart—pervades much of Wright's work, and it is the cause of the misunderstanding of Wright's genuine racial pride. Yet the vision in *Black Boy* is largely internally consistent; and *Black Boy*, one of the greatest American autobiographies, stands alongside those by Benjamin Franklin, Federick Douglass, Henry Adams, and Malcolm X.

As in *Native Son* and *The Outsider*, the inscription for *Black Boy* is taken from Job, which was apparently and expectedly Wright's favorite book of the Bible. "Why do the righteous suffer?" is not only Job's query but Wright's; and it is *the* question in *Black Boy*. Unremittingly secular, Wright finds no answer and no justice in the universe. The autobiography is his primal scream of protest at the cruelties inflicted on him not just by the white world, so forbidding and eager to keep him in his place, but also by the black one, from which he expected support, but from which he frequently got brutality and the same insistence on keeping in his place. Maternal lashings and adjurations to passivity (to break a too-pert spirit in order to camouflage it from white notice); the claustrophobic black church (so necessary to keep the community together by its offerings of law, guidance, fellowship, and the release of emotional tension); folk superstition (to soothe the curious human spirit that needs explanations in a society in which learning is barred)—all these drove the ambitious young Richard into a frenzy of resentment.

The following bitter passage, frequently cited as evidence of his lack of racial pride is instead testimony that Wright, as a middle-aged adult, strove mightily, by lashing out, to make sense of childhood experiences that were far too crushing to be assimilable by a youth or even by a young adult:

> (After I had outlived the shocks of childhood . . . I used to mull over the strange absence of real kindness in Negroes, how unstable was our tenderness, how lacking in genuine passion we were, how void of great hope, how timid our joy, how bare our traditions, how hollow our memories, and how shallow was even our despair. After I had learned other ways of life I used to brood upon the unconscious irony of those who felt Negroes led so passional an existence! I saw that what had been taken for our emotional strength was our negative confusions, our flights, our fears, our frenzy under pressure.
>
> (Whenever I thought of the essential bleakness of black life in America, I knew that Negroes had never been allowed to catch the full spirit of Western civilization, that they lived somehow in it but not of it. And when I brooded on the cultural barrenness of black life, I wondered if clean, positive tenderness, love, honor, loyalty, and the capacity to remember were native with man. I asked myself if these human qualities were not fostered, won, struggled and suffered for, preserved in a ritual from one generation to another. (45)

This initially strange-sounding attack, which is refuted both by the celebration of black culture in *Twelve Million Black Voices* as well as by an abundance of contrary assertion in *Black Boy*, is explained by Wright's remarkably strong personality, which allowed him to accomplish the near-impossible—to succeed; for that personality forced him at the same time to repudiate the culture whose cybernetics demanded no individuality. Though he was awestruck with praise for his race's success in forging its delicately balanced culture and then surviving and growing within it, when he thought of himself he viewed his black culture—so necessarily rife with preindividualist aspects—with antagonism because he found it devoid of values, beliefs, assumptions, traditions, and customs of a nature which he thought could have been of use to him in his struggle to excel. When he looked back on his youth, he felt his milieu was distinctive in the liberties it denied him and the narcosis (in the way of religious frenzy, sexual release, alcohol) with which it offered to replace them.

He could only feel affection for the culture, with its necessary strictures and inconsequential emotional releases, when at a distance from it,—when he considered it as a unity, as he did in *Twelve Million Black Voices*, rather than as an oppressing round hole in which he was a miserable (and misery-causing) square peg. Many black writers (Ralph Ellison and Houston A. Baker, Jr., for example) have insisted that they did not find black culture constricting or narrowing. But Wright was so extremely independent that it would have been hard for him in the late 1930s and early 1940s to have acknowledged that it was the black ethos which had helped make him a great writer—something his own environmentalist thinking should have forced him to admit. But he could never fully identify with any group, no matter how remarkable or unremarkable.

It is also probably true that the more he emphasizes what he considers the negative features of black culture, the more he stands out as exceptional in his hymn to himself, *Black Boy*. Although a reader does tire of his persistent self-pity and self-aggrandizement, Wright, without such a tough ego, would not have become such a remarkable man. And, of course, it is quite possible, as some critics assert, that he tended sometimes to see his own experience through white eyes; but, if he had been more critical of *every* aspect of white culture, he would have seen more positive values in his own black culture. He would, at any rate, have seen that many of his dissatisfactions were common to both races. For instance, he says of an incident involving his first piece of writing (a sketch of a doomed young Indian maiden) that, when he read it to a young woman who lived next door to him, she asked in perplexity what he was going to do with the sketch. "My environment contained nothing more alien than writing or the desire to express one's self in writing" (133). But he fails to acknowledge that, in this respect, black American and white American cultures correspond. He did not have the perspective to see that, like Nathaniel Hawthorne, Henry James, Ernest Hemingway, and so many other American writers, he was certain to feel alienated from the narrow, utilitarian values of most Americans, black and white.

Moreover, Wright's harsh lack of compassion for the black folk in the following observation seems equally shortsighted: "I saw a bleak, bare pool of black life and hated it; the people were alike, their homes were alike, and their farms were alike'' (151). Again, he fails to acknowledge that a dismal homogeneity is not monopolized by the black lower class; and he sometimes refuses to acknowledge the richness he inherited from his black community. But occasionally, even in *Black Boy*, he is able to assimilate the fact that his experiences as a youth were not all negative, and that the good ones are often directly related to his black heritage. Especially did his agrarian culture give to Wright a fondness for the natural world around him, its mystery and its wonder: ''There was a yearning for identification loosed in me by the sight of a solitary ant carrying a burden upon a mysterious journey'' (14).

The warm, nurturing black womanhood largely lacking in his early years but celebrated in *Twelve Million Black Voices* enriches his life in one of his first experiences in Memphis, when he is taken in as a boarder by a Mrs. Moss and her daughter Bess, who very simply and directly offers herself to him. (When Wright claims he was restrained with Bess, he is probably not entirely candid [*Quest*, 61].) What struck him particularly about his stay in Mrs. Moss's boardinghouse was the warmth and concern she evinced for him. Unwittingly, he once again offers evidence that contradicts his earlier claim about the lack of emotional stability in the black community. There are several other comparable passages that are internal evidence of his oneness with his race that have been sometimes overlooked by critics when they try to point out his alienation from it.

But it is indisputable that Wright's life was by and large mainly painful, a series of handicaps that he had to learn to use creatively rather than be disabled by them. The handicaps have been usefully divided into four categories by one of his biographers as being economic, familial, educational, and racial.[17] It was surely the racial one that had the most crucial consequences for him; for, to be born black in the Bottom South in 1908, one could be certain of being regarded as *nothing* by the predominant white society. Since no other writer, black or white, has overcome such formidable barriers to reach his goals, Wright will always be admired for his staggering achievement—and his admiration for himself in *Black Boy* is certainly understandable. Nothingness and its linguistic equivalent, silence, are what the South demanded of

Wright; but what it received was *Black Boy*.[18] Only in a strict chronological sense does the autobiography end with his young manhood; for, in terms of growth of consciousness and rage, it encompasses his entire life and career as surely as does *Twelve Million Black Voices*, the tender lay to his race and its agrarian roots.

IV *Invitation to Paris*

In *Black Boy* Wright narrated the events of his life through 1927. The publication of this book signaled the end of his best writing; for, although several critics have claimed that he did not subsequently decline as a writer, his best work was completed by 1945. After *Black Boy* appeared that year, Wright did not publish another book until 1953, when *The Outsider* appeared. Delivering speeches and engaging in debates, he became during this period of his career a public figure who was deeply saddened at America's returning to a consumerist ethic after World War II instead of its concentrating on racial problems. In the meantime, he witnessed many translations of *Black Boy*; began reviewing books; and during the fall of 1945, made a strenuous tour delivering lectures about the racial situation. The tour exhausted him so badly that he could not complete the scheduled fifty lectures. In addition to trying to fulfill his forensic obligations, he also in the fall of 1945 befriended and aided the black novelist Chester Himes by lending him money. And not only did he get James Baldwin a grant, but he also started him on his career. On January 12, 1946, he attended Countee Cullen's funeral. Having accepted an invitation from the French government, he sailed for France on May 1. In Paris he was feted and lionized during the month of May. In November he and Ellen went to Switzerland, where he gave some interviews and contacted a publisher for the German edition of *Black Boy*. At the end of 1946, he met George Padmore, the father of African liberation.

From the summer of 1946 until his death in the fall of 1960, France was his home base, although he traveled extensively. These last fourteen years are notable for a change in his ideological emphases: instead of determinism, he explored choice; instead of racism, he emphasized a more metaphysical isolation; in place of colonialism in the Deep South, he concentrated on global oppression. Existentialism and Third Worldism are outgrowths of his earlier experiences; and, while he was no longer a member of the Communist party, his writings during these years as an exile show the retention of his Marxist ideals and sympathies.

In January 1947, when the Wrights returned to Manhattan and moved into a house on Charles Street, Wright had trouble becoming readjusted to America, and he wrote little after his return from France. Because the pressure of American racism grew intense, he left for France again in the summer of 1947; but, even when resettled in Paris, he still had trouble writing. Contrary to the common view, there may well be no cause-and-effect relationship between his leaving America for France and the decline of quality in his work, for the quality might have declined if he had remained in America.

Wright's dream of finding fulfillment in Europe ended after a year or two, as Fabre indicates: "He had come to France to find a humanist tradition; he thought he had found it in 1946, only to have it retreat in 1948 before the advances of Americanization" (*Quest*, 326). He worked with the philosopher Jean-Paul Sartre to make the non-Communist Rassemblement Démocratique Révolutionnaire a strong political movement for individualism and humanism. In addition to this work, Wright also gave interviews, lectured, attended parties, and, in general, made little progress with *The Outsider*—Fabre mentions "a sort of repugnance to finish his novel" (*Quest*, 334).

In 1949, when his second daughter, Rachel, was born in Paris, he spent much of his time working on the film version of *Native Son*. During the filming in Argentina, Wright, like most foreigners in Perón's country, was subject to police surveillance. After the picture was finished in October 1950, the version shown in the United States underwent radical surgery to comply with the censors. Although Wright considered this film "a total disaster" (*Quest*, 351), and although he made no money on it, he still retained his interest in film-making. In order to play the role of Bigger Thomas, the middle-aged Wright, a little pudgy even after all the years of undernourishment, had to diet.

After the demise of the Rassemblement Démocratique Révolutionnaire, Wright put his efforts into the French-American Fellowship, an organization which wanted to establish a more realistic relationship between America and France than existed in 1950 and to combat racism in American businesses abroad. By the end of 1951 the fellowship no longer functioned; but Wright's dedication during his tenure as president was impressive—and so time-consuming that it prevented his completely devoting his thoughts to *The Outsider*. Another impediment to its rapid completion was his unfortunate quarrel with Baldwin; for, although Wright had been nettled by his protégé's first essay on *Native Son*, he became infuriated by a subsequent one, which he perceived as a hostile attempt by the young artist to assert his own integrity at Wright's expense. Finally, in London in early 1952, during a three-month period, he completed *The Outsider* after almost six years of work. It was published in 1953, the year he wrote *Savage Holiday* (1954), which appeared as a paperback original and is the least regarded of his five published novels.

He next began a period of wanderlust: "Wright did not actually leave France [yet], but 1953 seems to mark his spiritual departure from Paris and Europe" (*Quest*, 383). Because he was led to research and write nonfictional works based on his travels, he sailed in June 1953 for Ghana, which was then called the Gold Coast. Dissatisfied because of his inability to fathom tribal culture, he left the Gold Coast in early September;—however, by the spring of 1954, he had finished writing the book inspired by his trip, *Black Power* (1954). In October, when he spoke in Amsterdam about the liberation movement in the Gold Coast, he met at the reception his Dutch translator, Margrit de Sablonière, who became a close personal friend.

In the meantime, while he was looking for another country to analyze in a book, he remembered Gertrude Stein's advice to see Spain and eventually decided to go there. He began his trip by car in August 1954, but returned to Paris in September; however, since he was convinced that he could write an original book on Spain if he returned there, he did so in November.

Early the following year, he prepared to attend the Bandung Conference, a meeting of the Third World. The Congress for Cultural Freedom, formed to denounce tyranny and later revealed as financed indirectly by the Central Intelligence Agency, agreed to pay his travel expenses to Indonesia. The product of this trip was *The Color Curtain*, which was finished in June 1955. In the fall of 1955 he began work on a novel tentatively called "Mississippi," which he worked on sporadically until it was published as *The Long Dream* in 1958 as the intended first novel in a projected trilogy; the second, "Island of Hallucinations," has been published only as excerpts.

He took part in the planning of the First Congress of Negro Artists and Writers, which was held in Paris in September 1956. At the conference he spoke about the differences between Africans and Afro-Americans; and he questioned the value of tribal culture in Africa's attempt to throw off the effects of imperialism. "The Congress was almost an intellectual Bandung for Wright, who called upon his colleagues to reject a useless past and to turn toward rationalism and industrialization" (*Quest*, 438). Needless to say, many of the African delegates found this position offensive. On November 22, 1956, he began a lecture tour of Scandinavia where, in Copenhagen, he received the original inspiration for "Big Good Black Man"; and late in this same year he finished *White Man, Listen!*, a collection of four essays.

The same year he also translated Louis Sapin's play *Papa Bon Dieu* (Daddy Goodness), which reflects his persistent interest in black folk culture, specifically in the cults of Father Divine and Daddy Grace. The play was never performed in Wright's lifetime, but it did appear in an off-Broadway theater in 1969. In the autumn of 1956 Wright was secure in his literary reputation, financial status, and social position in France. "It is therefore somewhat surprising that he was so profoundly affected by some unfortunate occurrences that he could not regain enough peace of mind to continue writing for quite a long time" (*Quest*, 447). One reason for his distress was the death of Aunt Maggie, his mother's sister and one of the few people he had been close to in his childhood. Another incident that disturbed him was the printed attack on him by a reporter named Ben Burns in the March 8, 1956, *Reporter*: "By 1957, Wright began to consider all attacks against him as part of a general plot, and since later incidents tend to support this theory it would not be difficult to agree with him" (*Quest*, 450). By the summer of 1957 he had to pay some attention to financial matters, and he was additionally depressed by the negative reviews of *White Man, Listen!* and by the same early negativism in the reviews of *The Long Dream*.

Since the beginning of 1959, he had wanted to write a book on French-speaking Africa that would be comparable to *Black Power.* At first he considered enlisting the financial aid of the American Society for African Culture to support his proposed tour of Senegal, Mauritania, Sudan, Guinea, the Ivory Coast, Nigeria, and Upper Volta, but this scheme did not work, for "sickness, lack of money and finally death prevented him from realizing this project which meant so much to him" (*Quest*, 491). In 1959 he also planned to move to London because France was falling more and more under the hand of de Gaulle and because of the attacks on the expatriate Afro-American writers in France.

After a party in 1959 to mark the publication of the French translation of *White Man, Listen!*, Wright became sick from an attack of amoebic dysentery, contracted probably during his travels in the Gold Coast. When he visited England this same year, he was still fighting amoebic dysentery and, by February 1960, he was ill all the time. He became very good friends with his doctor, Victor Schwartzmann, who treated him without charge because of his admiration for his work. In the same month, when Wright learned that the stage adaptation of *The Long Dream* had received such bad reviews that its performance was stopped by its adapter, Ketti Frings, he viewed the negative reviews of the New York drama critics as aimed at him personally.

In the meantime he was sorely pressed financially, since he had to keep an apartment for himself in Paris and one for his family in London. Although he was in need of rest, he had to work because of his financial problems; and, although he was supposed to be revising "Island of Hallucinations," he could not make himself work on it. The summer of 1959 was spent in writing a long short story, "Leader Man," that remains unpublished. He wanted to start a serious crime magazine, to be called *Crime International*, and he also planned the collection of short stories that, by January 18, 1960, was entitled *Eight Men.*

On March 19, 1960, he told his Dutch translator, Margrit de Sablonière, that he was writing poetry—*haiku*; and his writing in this delicate poetical form seems to have been therapy for his illness, loneliness, and fear of personal attack. He selected enough poems from the 4,000 *haiku* he wrote for a volume, which was rejected by World Publishers and has not subsequently been published, although some of the individual poems have appeared. Throughout the last summer of his life, he worked on an unpublished short story, "The Law of a Father," in which the relationship between the father and his son may echo a sad event in Wright's own life: a Swedish girl named Bente Heeris told him, after reading *Native Son* and *Black Boy*, of her decision to kill herself; he was not able to prevent her. After his death, three other books by Wright appeared: *Eight Men* (1961), *Lawd Today* (1963), and *American Hunger* (1977).

During this final period of his life, he was in such need of money that for a while he wrote copy for record jackets, and he became so suspicious of people that he even distrusted friends like Dr. Schwartzmann. On November 8, 1960, when he gave a lecture at the American Church in Paris, he attacked the spying in the black community. On November 26 he went to the Eugene Gibez Clinic, where Dr. Schwartzmann advised him to convalesce; but he died of a heart attack during the late evening of November 28. "Various questions were raised by his sudden death" (*Quest*, 521). Although Fabre "was unable to discover the slightest proof that Wright had been assassinated. . . , I [Fabre] could not automatically conclude that Wright had not been the victim of the 'evil designs' of the CIA" (*Quest*, 522). Since the body was cremated on December 3, a medical examination was impossible. Fabre hypothesizes that racism itself may have created such inner tensions that it helped cause Wright's death and he suggests another possible cause: "I myself [Fabre] do not consider it unreasonable to conclude that a series of provocations was directed against Wright by the American government and that these were to a certain extent responsible for his heart attack" (*Quest*, 524).

CHAPTER 2

His Apprenticeship

I *Urban Nihilism*

POSTHUMOUSLY published in 1963, *Lawd Today* was probably written between 1931 and 1937 (*Quest,* 626), when Wright was living in Chicago. "The title *Lawd Today*, a folk exclamation on confronting the events of the day, is to express a people who have not been able to make their life their own, who must live 'from day to day.' "[1] In this work Wright narrates the day of February 12, 1937, in the life of Jake Jackson, a black postal clerk. Wright's debt to James Joyce's *Ulysses* is obvious, for Joyce also recounted the events of one day in the life of his protagonist. Jake's day is emblematic of his entire existence—hopeless, squalid, pointless, ugly. Since he is an unaccommodated man, the facts and conditions of his existence preclude any but the briefest illusions of significance. From the minute he wakes up until the time he passes out in a drunken stupor the following morning, his life is a vacuum that will never be even partially filled. Having migrated "Up South," he still refuses to acknowledge that the racial barriers in the North are almost as formidable, and certainly more subtle, than those in the Deep South. Rather than the Promised Land, his surroundings are an extension of the Southern nightmare.

Like *Native Son*, *Lawd Today* opens with a noise which awakens the protagonist. Bigger rises to the "brriinng" of an alarm clock; Jake, to the eight o'clock "ting" on the radio on February 12, 1937, the one-hundred-twenty-eighth anniversary of the birthday of the president described by the radio announcer as the one who "bestowed the blessings of liberty and freedom upon millions of his fellowmen."[2] This description is only one of the many brutal ironies in Wright's work; for Jake, who is still a slave, has the illusion of having freedom. Moreover, he is not aware that Lincoln had "freed" the slaves only in the rebellious Southern states over which he had no authority. Without realizing the irony of his situation, Jake thinks, "*I'm just like a slave*" (21); and he does so on Lincoln's birthday.

Before Jake awakens fully, he has a dream, one of Wright's favorite devices. In his nightmare, a voice reminiscent of his boss yells at him to climb an endless series of steps; but, when he runs faster, he makes no progress. His dream not only is a prelude to his day and his future; it is also the history of black people in America. This dream is Wright's equivalent of the incident in Ralph Ellison's *Invisible Man* in which the nameless protagnoist learns that he is to be kept running, running.

Jake is extremely earthy, animalistic, even bestial, as he scratches and gropes around his body. He treats his wife, Lil, as a subhuman, the way Bigger treats Bessie, his "girlfriend." He throws her Christian magazine across the room since he, again like Bigger, has little use for Christianity. He owes everyone; and, although he tries to blame his financial woes on his wife, many of them are his fault. Lil, suffering from a tumor, needs a $1000 operation, which he cannot afford and would like to avoid (since the novel covers only a single twenty-four-hour period, the reader never learns if Jake finally allows her the medical treatment). One also learns that, if Lil complains about Jake's repulsive behavior to the post office once more, her husband will be fired. Their marriage is a fraud, for he would never have married Lil if she had not told him that she was pregnant and that he was the father. His treatment of her is utterly brutal: he slaps her, kicks her, breaks her arm. James Baldwin charges that, where sex should be in Wright's fiction, there is only violence; but Eldridge Cleaver's rejoinder is convincing: he explains that, because of America's brutalization of blacks, violence does indeed reign on the holy throne of sex.

Jake's lack of knowledge about himself and everything else is pathetic: it takes him some considerable time to calculate that twelve multiplied by five equals sixty; he tortures himself in one of the few light touches in the book when he tries to comb out the kinks in his hair; he reveals through his reactions to the newspaper headlines he glances at that he is a Republican (a worshiper at the shrine of money), a racist (he hates Germans and Jews), an admirer of gangsters, an anti-Communist. (When Wright wrote *Lawd Today*, he probably intended Jake's anticommunism as evidence for his ignorance; years later, though, his revised version of this early fiction, *The Outsider*, shows how anticommunist Wright himself had become, although his anticommunism was based on personal experience and although he kept Marxist sympathies.) Jake's mind, the narrator explains, is "lost in a warm fog" (36), an apt figure for a man with no visibility in a society he himself does not clearly perceive. His imperception makes him so gullible that he takes seriously advertising circulars that claim their products will cure alcoholism, backache, and impotency. Even when the burning truth is before his eyes—a picture "of a nude, half-charred body of a Negro swinging from the end of a rope" (41)—he ignores it. Jake seems incapable of acknowledging his real place in American society.

Thinking a dream he had has something to do with numbers, he goes to the Black Gold Policy Wheel, which is delighted to take his money. His bet placed, then lost, he can find nothing better to do with his time than goggle blankly at movie posters. When he sees a poster advertising a movie about flying, Jake, like the would-be pilot Bigger Thomas, thinks, "*Being a aviator sure must be fun, 'specially when you on top of another plane and can send it spinning down like that*" (50). In *The Wretched of the Earth*, Frantz Fanon has pointed out how the oppressed dream about running, jumping, flying, all activities that suggest mobility, something Jake does not have.

Later, at Doc Higgins's Tonsorial Palace, where Jake meets Duke, who is apparently an unemployed Communist, Jake and Doc Higgins both scorn Duke's communism as a method of improving the lot of the black man. Jake tells him, " 'Nigger, you'd last as long trying to overthrow the government as a fart in a wind storm!' " (54). He endorses the platitudinous contention that " 'niggers is just like a bunch of crawfish in a bucket, the others'll grab hold on 'im and pull 'im back . . .' " (55). Jake and Doc Higgins agree that Booker T. Washington's method is the best way to "climb out of the bucket"; but neither Jake nor his barber realize that Washington had emphasized material values almost to the total exclusion of racial and human ones. After hearing more tributes to Lincoln on the radio, Jake and Doc concur that the Great Emancipator was an exceptional man.

By now it is nine o'clock, and Jake has three hours of nothingness to endure before he must suffer through eight more hours of doing the repetitive, boring, "nothing" work at the post office. Because he has never been in a library, he considers that possibility but decides not to enter; for, after all, reading books will merely addle his brains. Instead, he decides to visit his pal Bob, a fellow employee at the post office, who has venereal disease and a wife who is demanding alimony from him. At his friend's apartment, Jake's quiddity is summed up when he is described as "pleasantly vacuous" (66). After two more of Jake's cronies arrive at Bob's—Slim, who has tuberculosis, and Al, a grossly overweight sergeant in the National Guard—a four-way staccato dialogue ensues in which the speakers are not explicitly identified for many lines at a time. Although the use of verticality (passages of dialogue in which speakers are not explicitly identified and remarks are brief, resulting in a narrow column in the center of the page) indicates a possible debt to Hemingway, dialogue is one of Wright's fortes; and it is, perhaps, the most impressive part of his achievement in *Lawd Today*. The quartet plays bridge, but Slim's violent coughing interrupts and undercuts the fun. "Jake's mind fished about, trying to get hold of an idea to cover his feeling of uneasy emptiness" (79). Insofar as Jake can be said to have a mind, it is usually blank. A bout of the "dozens" (an Afro-American word game used also by Wright in *Uncle Tom's Children* and in *Black Boy* in which the intent is to insult the opponent's mother, without losing one's composure when one's own mother is insulted) between Al and Jake affords Bob and Slim and the reader considerable delight (80-81).

When the time is 10:45, Jake still has over an hour to kill. He and his friends consume some more time listening gullibly to a mountebank who is selling a panacea for physical ailments. Wright summarizes the four men's mindless acceptance of platitudes when Al says, " 'A stitch in time saves nine' " (88). The narrator then takes the opportunity to satirize Marcus Garvey and the back-to-Africa movement as the four clerks watch a parade go by: "These were the supreme generals of a mythical African republic, and the medals of unfought wars and unwon victories clinked against their uniforms with every rattle of drums" (93). The refusal to indulge in romantic fantasies is typical of Wright and it informs all his writing, including *Lawd Today*. Anticipating the authors of the 1960s who take pride in black physical characteristics, Wright chafes to see people refuse to accept what they are: "They passed a beauty parlor and the scent of burning hair stung their nostrils. From a doorway a black woman stepped to the sidewalk and came briskly forward. Her hair was shining jet, and was brushed straight back, plastered to her head. The contrast between the overdose of white powder and the natural color of her skin was so sharp that she looked like two people instead of one; it was as if her ghost were walking in front of her" (95; see 120 also).

Since all four men are from the South, they are consequently part of the Great Migration to the urban North and, in this case, to Chicago. Although the North's destruction of black folk culture is not so complete as in William Attaway's *Blood on the Forge*, the devastation is nevertheless severe. Jake and his companions cannot bear to accept what they are: the product of 300 years of oppression; a remnant whose feudal, rural way of life has been replaced by an industrial, urban one. As a result, no adjustments have been made. As the "L" train takes them to the post office, where they will do work that is stupefyingly monotonous, they stare at the forbidden fruit: a white woman's exposed thighs.

The epigraph for Part Two, "Squirrel's Cage," which is from Waldo Frank's *Our America*—"Now, when you study these long, rigid rows of desiccated men and women, you feel that you are in the presence of some form of life that has hardened but not grown, and over which the world has passed"—is an appropriate inscription for Jake and thousands of his urban brothers. The Chicago Post Office, where Jake and Cross Damon (the protagonist in *The Outsider*) act like squirrels in a cage, is "a huge, dark grey building, almost the color of the sky, occupying a square block":

Just to look at it depressed Jake. A sudden sense of all the weary hours he had spent within those blackened walls filled him with foreboding. As he mounted the steps, he wondered if he would have to go on this way year after year 'til he died. Was this *all*? Deep in him was a dumb yearning for something else; somewhere or other was something or other

> for him. But where? How? All he could see right now was an endless stretch of black postal days; and all he could feel was the agony of standing on his feet till they ached and sweated, of breathing dust till he spat black, of jerking his body when a voice yelled. (101-102)

Even in the Depression year of 1936, the white clerks regard their jobs as temporary; but no black man doubts that a job at the post office is as much as he can expect. At noon Jake begins to work on a "job" that pays $2,100 a year, the same job he has had for over eight years, and one that he feels he must keep. When Lil again complains to the post office authorities about him, he is saved from being fired by Doc Higgins's influence, for which he pays $75. The working conditions in the post office are not dissimilar to those in a penitentiary: "At intervals a foreman makes rounds of inspection to see that all is going well. Under him works a legion of cat-footed spies and stool pigeons who snoop eternally. Along the walls are slits through which detectives peep and peer" (113). The ambience of the post office, reflecting that of the book as a whole, is one of futility, pointlessness, ignorance, stupidity, disgust.

After a shouting match with his section manager because of eight misthrown letters, Jake wishes the white head of the Statue of Liberty would fall from being hit by a shell from a battleship manned by a black crew. Since Wright's protagonists often attack their victims' heads, this act suggests that the ultimate problem they face is a mental one, one in people's heads. While working, Jake and his friends do everything they can to escape facing reality, but the environment of the post office persistently intrudes. Jake gives a semblance of interest in something when Al asks him to join the National Guard, the function of which distresses neither man: " 'Ain't nothing to it, Jake. Look, when the Reds start something, we put 'em down, see? If some guys think they can strike and tie up things, we stop 'em, see? If riots break out, we's right on hand, see? Boy, you should have heard the speech the Governor handed us last week. It was a pip. And JEEEsus, you get *paid* for it! And here's something that's right down your alley; when you get into any trouble in the Post Office, they ain't as hard on you as they is when you ain't a soljer . . .' " (132). Such casualness toward social responsibility is repeated in Jake's personal life, for the reader learns that Jake tricked Lil into having an abortion by a quack doctor when she was seventeen; and, because the operation was not performed correctly, she had to go to a hospital.

While the four men temporarily relieve their boredom by telling dirty jokes, a white clerk eavesdrops, which infuriates them: " 'They [white people] never want to have nothing to do with us, but when we's talking about women they's always sticking their damn noses in' " (136-37). The external environment complements the hostility of the inner one; for outside the post office the wind howls "like a lost dog in a vast wilderness" (137). Even Jake's few superficial human values are negated by the impinging universe, because the four men tend to regard the white world as a predominating reality and environment. In one conversation they reveal their own sense of profound inferiority and what they consider to be the white world's superiority (144). When they then exchange one platitude after another, their language is as devoid of content as the milieu. Although there is some *Native Son* talk, these four vacuums never really act upon it:

". . . and the white folks stoned a little black boy and drowned 'im 'cause he was swimming in the wrong part of the lake."

"Now, ain't that a bitch! Swimming in the *wrong* part of the lake. . . ."

". . . and the lake is *miles* big."

"That's as bad as killing a man for breathing."

"I wonder is there anything a white man won't do?"

"They make us live in one corner of the city. . . ."

". . . like we was some kind of wild animals. . . ."

". . . then they make us pay anything they want to for rent. . . ."

" 'cause we can't live nowhere but where they tell us!"

"I remember when they use' to run us out of our homes with bombs."

"Even when you's dead, they tell you where to go."

"Lawd, today! Jim Crow *graveyards*!" (149)

But, for the most part, the empty, pointless, trivial chatter that lightens the burden and boredom of their stultifying work reveals their own vacuity: they are nonmen.

Concurring that the North is an improvement over the South, they nevertheless retain some pleasant but possibly overly idealized memories of the pleasures enjoyed Down South. In particular, they have memories of their hunting and swimming—activities abrogated by their urban environment. Part Two terminates with laughter by the four men at some obscene pictures of men and women in different positions of sexual intercourse; and the reader learns that these pictures are one of the high points of their day from the four men's excited chatter.

The epigraph to Part Three, "Rat's Alley," is taken from T. S. Eliot's *The Waste Land*: "But at my back in a cold blast I hear/The rattle of the bones, and chuckle spread from ear to ear." From Part III of Eliot's poem, which is concerned with sex without love, this twentieth-century version of Andrew Marvell's coy mistress informs the end of the novel, in which love is just another sordid means of gaining the tawdry excitement which is a deliverance from boredom. On their way to Rose's, a combination night club and whorehouse, Jake and his three friends read about another lynching in the South; and one of them remarks that a black man who does not have enough sense to leave the South ought to be lynched.

At Rose's, they try to blot out the experience of working in the post office by venting emotional energy through eating, dancing, yelling, sex. The atmosphere at Rose's is orgiastic:

> Abruptly, the dance changed; her [a dancing woman's] legs leaped into the air; her body ran riot with a goal of its own. The muscles of her stomach rose and fell insatiably. The music whirled faster and she whirled faster. She seemed possessed by the impelling excitement of her nervous system. The climax came when she clasped her knees together in a steel-like clamp and wrapped her arms tightly around her heaving bosom. She trembled from head to feet, her face distorted in orgiastic agony. A thin black woman grabbed her boy friend and bit his ear till blood came. (177)

Jake's money, which he had just borrowed from the post office, is stolen; when he accuses his partner, Blanche (the name may be used symbolically to suggest white economic exploitation), of being in on the robbery, he is beaten by Blue Juice and the latter's friends. Jake then stumbles home to a vicious brawl with Lil. After a night of being robbed and beaten, and after later being cut by his wife, he passes out in a drunken stupor. Outside, the wind whines and moans "like an idiot in a deep black pit" (189); and that wind is like Jake himself.

In *Lawd Today* Wright is a thoroughgoing environmentalist and determinist. Jake and his friends are in all respects the inevitable products of an environment that completely explains them.

Jake has no hope in the present or the future, in this life or in the problematical next one; and he has no choices to make. Although critics have given the novel extreme judgments by evaluating it either as excellent or as terrible, neither view is correct, for this apprentice novel is competently done but is neither particularly good nor bad. It is thin; it does not have the resonance or moral power of *Black Boy* or *Native Son*; but it does render compellingly the conversation, the ambience, the sights of the black ghetto of Chicago as it existed and exists. *Lawd Today* successfully conveys the sordidness, the futility, the nihilism of black urban experience.

II *Harriet Beecher Stowe's Progeny*

Wright's first book to be published, *Uncle Tom's Children*, is a different matter altogether from *Lawd Today*. Originally published in 1938, the collection reappeared in 1940 with two additions: an autobiographical essay, "The Ethics of Living Jim Crow," and a fifth short story, "Bright and Morning Star." In *Uncle Tom's Children* Wright uses the setting where Jake Jackson's forebears grew up: a highly traditional, rural, southern, preindustrial, preindividualist culture—a culture that above all kept the black man "in his place." The book suggests, though, that Uncle Tom is dead.

The autobiographical essay, "The Ethics of Living Jim Crow," with which the 1940 edition opens, is *Black Boy* in miniature. The choice for a black person in the South is simple, for as Wright indicates in this essay, he can either physically exist as a "nigger" or live briefly as a black man but die. The first incident in Wright's learning such Jim Crow ethics was when he dared to fight back against white boys. Expecting his mother to approve of him, he finds instead that she beats him until he has a temperature of a hundred and two; and this episode is an early indication of the source of Wright's ambivalent feelings toward his mother. The price of survival is emasculation: black culture punished its men for being men. In the days of slavery, a black man, in order to survive, had to stand passively by while white men violated his wife, daughters, and sisters; and even by Wright's day, many blacks perceived the same necessity of trading away action against societal wrongs in return for a normal black life span. But it was extremely painful for Wright to acknowledge that black culture had to enforce a considerable degree of outward conformity to white expectations in order for blacks to survive; consequently, unwilling to adapt permanently, he had to leave the South or die.

In recording his shocked amazement at this maternal endorsement of racial passivity, Wright may well feign more naiveté than he really had. Many incidents in "The Ethics of Living Jim Crow," as in *Black Boy*, reveal an innocent, sensitive, inexperienced young black man who is set against a stereotypically cruel world. Wright is always willing to see himself as wronged and to view the world, white and black, as evil. This priggish attitude is offensive, but it does allow him to score his points in a crudely powerful way. His pose as Galahad does not qualify the essential truth, however; and, besides, he is not a newspaper reporter who is baldly conveying facts but an imaginative artist.

"Big Boy Leaves Home" is the first and best short story in the collection. The title is pregnant with irony: Big Boy does not "leave"—he flees in order to survive; and it is not "home" that he abandons but racial perdition. Treated as a "big boy" by the whites, the protagonist is shocked into manhood by watching three murders and by killing one person himself. The four innocent black adolescents one sees at the beginning of the story roll on the warm earth and engage in a bout of the dozens in what seems to be an Edenic setting. The only suggestion of flight from this garden is the mournful whistle of a train in the distance; this sound is a prelusion of Big Boy's sudden escape to the North, which, as *Native Son* dramatizes, will not be a Promised Land or Glory.

As in *Lawd Today*, the conversation of *Uncle Tom's Children* is marked by verticality; for the speakers, whether Buck, Bobo, Lester, or Big Boy, are often unidentified. When the other three start for the water hole to go swimming, Big Boy objects, afraid they will be lynched. They engage in some playful but serious wrestling to settle the difference. Big Boy, through strength and shrewdness, overcomes his three opponents and, feeling strong and cocky, decides he will, after all, accompany them swimming. He victoriously brags, " 'Yuh see . . . when a ganga guys jump on yuh, all yuh gotta do is put the heat on one of them n make im tell the others t let up, see?' "[3] Big Boy's first "cowardly" instincts that warned against a dip in the water hole were the correct ones, and his adolescent braggadocio ultimately and ironically comes to mean that the whites need only to lynch one black to repress the whole community because in doing so they terrorize all blacks.

When the black boys reach the swimming hole, they ignore old man Harvey's no trespassing sign and cross into the white world which they are prohibited by custom and law from entering. They take off their clothes and throw them "in a pile under a tree" (24). "Sending up silver spray in the sunlight," Bobo and Big Boy are pushed into the water (25); and the description here is almost the same as that when Buck is shot: "he toppled headlong, sending up a shower of bright spray into the sunlight" (29). The beauty of nature remains the same whether man sees the world as idyllic or nightmarish. After the swimming and the horseplay, the quartet emerges from the water to rest and to dry; they still entertain vaguely the possibility that old man Harvey might appear; and a northbound train whistles in the distance, just before the forbidden fruit in this southern Hesperides is about to appear. Events contradict the expectations that are caused by their environment:

> They grew pensive. A black winged butterfly hovered at the water's edge. A bee droned. From somewhere came the sweet scent of honeysuckles. Dimly they could hear sparrows twittering in the woods. They rolled from side to side, letting sunshine dry their skins and warm their blood. They plucked blades of grass and chewed them.
>
> "Oh!"
>
> A white woman, poised on the edge of the opposite embankment, stood directly in front of them, her hat in her hand and her hair lit by the sun.
>
> "Its a woman!" whispered Big Boy in an underbreath. "A *white* woman!"
>
> They stared, their hands instinctively covering their groins. (27)

The sexual myths and fantasies so potent in black-white confrontations begin to inform the story in a powerful way from this point onward. The four young blacks know the white man has denied them access to this pale Eve, and they know also that, to white eyes, the circumstances will generate only one interpretation: sexual molestation of the flower of southern womanhood by depraved, brutalized, black beasts. That the white woman, Bertha, "backed away to the tree where their clothes lay in a heap" (28) is important; for, instead of running away, she puts herself in such a position that the young black men have to follow her in order to get their clothes; the sexual implications are provocative.[4]

At this point, Wright's sheer narrative energy assumes control; for, before the reader can assimilate events, a white man, Jim, has shot and killed Buck and Lester; Big Boy has shot and killed Jim; and Big Boy and Bobo flee to get "home," not realizing they *are* "home" as far as their place in America is concerned. All this violence occurs because four adolescents decided to go swimming; violence is always the principal reality in a black man's existence in America. It has been suggested that, in "Big Boy Leaves Home," "changes in the physical environment accompany, heighten, and correspond to changes in the narrative line, particularly at critical moments. It should be added that Wright effects this discreetly and unobtrusively, well within the boundaries of realism; nowhere is there a hint of the pathetic fallacy."[5] Good examples of this observation occur when Big Boy and Bobo are desperately fleeing: a pastoral nature becomes cruel as vines and leaves scratch Bobo (30) and corn stubbles bruise their feet (31).

After Big Boy reaches his house, the black community, pre-individualist, must decide what to do with this example of individual self-assertion. Mrs. Morrison, Big Boy's mother, gives the Christian solution: only God can help her son now. Similar to what Bigger Thomas's mother thinks, this attitude was always detested by Wright, for religious passivity and rejection of the secular world were condemned by him. Finally, the men of the community decide Big Boy should hide while waiting for a truck that is to be driven by one of the men's sons and bound for Chicago, for Canaan. That Big Boy will hide underground is significant because the underground man is one of Wright's controlling metaphors that presides not only over all his major work but even in his own life. Once a black man has acted like a man, gained visibility, he must again become literally invisible to white eyes in order to survive. But the predominant point to be made is that Uncle Tom's children fight back when threatened.

Baldwin's observation that Wright's great forte was dramatizing internal states by means of externals is true in this story: "A light wind skipped over the grass. A beetle hit on his [Big Boy's] cheek and he brushed it off. Behind the dark pines hung a red sun. Two bats flapped against that sun. He shivered, for he was growing cold; the sweat on his body was drying" (41). Wright is good at linking scenery with states of mind: Big Boy's inner fears and forebodings are reflected, advertised, and suggested by the outer world just as it reinforces changes in the narrative line. The hostility of the environment persists as Big Boy looks for a suitable underground kiln to hide in: a six-foot rattlesnake coils in one of them. Having killed this snake, he backs slowly into the dark hole: "When inside he felt there must be snakes about him, ready to strike. It seemed he could see and feel them there, waiting tensely in coil. In the dark he imagined long, white fangs ready to sink into his neck, his side, his legs. He wanted to come out, but kept still. Shucks, he told himself, ef there wuz any snakes in here they sho woulda done bit me by now. Some of his fear left, and he relaxed" (42). The implication is that Big Boy's plight represents the way blacks in America feel as they hide underground.

For the fourth time Big Boy hears a train whistle, and this time it makes him remember how he and his three friends of the past used to pretend they were riding locomotives when they played on the hillside. Now Big Boy's dreams will be realized, but hardly in a way he had envisioned. This story is basically, then, a *bildungsroman*, for the uninitiated is forced to acknowledge the real nature of the world through a violent confrontation with it. Big Boy indulges another fantasy while he sits waiting for Bobo to join him: he imagines himself shooting white men as they charge up the hill. The reality, of course, has no relation to his wish-fulfillment, for the reality is that Bobo is about to be lynched. "The lynching here emerges as a dramatic ceremony in which Negroes occupy the center of the sexual life of the white community."[6] The atmosphere is casual and sometimes even gay; a lynching is like a carnival at which the souvenirs are parts of Bobo instead of stuffed pandas. Big Boy truly has left home when he sees Bobo tarred and feathered, then burned to death. Lynching. which symbolizes the relationship between the white and black communities in the Deep South, is a basic motif in Wright's fiction; he wrote a poem about it, "Between the World and Me," and there is a really gruesome picture of a lynching in *Twelve Million Black Voices.* Big Boy survives only because it begins to rain. A dog discovers him, but he is able to kill it, again suggesting existence for blacks is a matter of survival, not of self-realization. Big Boy rides north in a truck, perhaps to become another Bigger Thomas.

Wright so based this story on actual events that Constance Webb has observed that it "contains a description of the creek in which Wright swam with his friends."[7] The lynching itself is based on that of Bob Robinson, a childhood acquaintance, while other details are "based on information he had collected from David Poindexter," a friend from his days of membership in the Communist party in Chicago.[8] Although Wright has often been accused of sensationalism, the historical record indicates that he is, if anything, restrained in his depiction of Bobo's lynching. If violence, particularly burning and hanging, permeates Wright's fiction, it does so because of Afro-American experiences in the art of survival.

The ensuing story, "Down by the Riverside," is not so impressive as "Big Boy Leaves Home" when judged in respect to the moral-aesthetic power that it generates. Taking its ironic title from a popular song of the same name, the story is concerned with Southern blacks who face not only racial hatred but also hostile nature, for the hero, who is perhaps too obviously named Mann, must save his family from flood waters while simultaneously taking his fatally pregnant wife, Lulu, to the hospital. It is difficult to resist the temptation of seeing Mann as a modern analogue to the earlier man, Noah. The interweaving of natural and racial turmoil begins with the tale's earliest events, for Mann's brother Bob, sent out for a boat with which to save the family from the rising floodwaters, returns with a stolen one which, like its original owner, is white—and that color is used persistently in Wright's fiction as a symbol for danger, menace. That Wright had an Existentialist's interest in boundary situations a decade before he had met Jean-Paul Sartre is clear from Bob's remark to Mann as he prepares to evacuate the family: " 'Yuhll be rowin ergin the current ever inch [of the way to the Red Cross

Hospital], n wid a boat full itll be the Devil t pay. The watahs twelve foot deep n flowin strong n tricky' " (60).

Wright's rigorous secularism percolates through the narrative when the flatulent Brother Murray prays and sings instead of helping in a more practical way; he does, however, take some of Mann's potential passengers off his hands, although at no danger to himself, because he leaves before Mann, when the floodwaters are still relatively low. And then, like Big Boy and the author himself, Mann finds himself alone, separated from the black community and, indeed, from mankind, as he tries to navigate the stolen rowboat to the hospital. Wright's fictional heroes are ultimately cosmic exiles who, in their aloneness and isolation, embody the anguish that is a part of every human's life.

All readers of "Down by the Riverside" have noticed a most conspicuous coincidence in Wright's arrangement of the narrative: Mann asks for help at the house of Heartfield, who is also the white owner of Mann's boat. Since Wright's narrative is representational, this incident violates credibility, but it allows him to make a point: the line between tract and art is often trespassed here and elsewhere, most notably in *Native Son*. Mann is forced to shoot and kill Heartfield when the latter tries to kill him. Although violence is the mode of intercourse between blacks and whites, Uncle Tom's children now defend themselves.

Even in death, the blacks have no dignity to the whites. At the hospital the doctor, the nurses, the colonel, all white, are either mildly discomfited by or completely insensitive to Lulu's dying. They force Mann to help fight the floodwaters, although he is tired and although his wife has just died. Most of the white characters in *Uncle Tom's Children* are portrayed as stereotypical monsters because they are presented in the stories as they are seen through the eyes of the black characters, who have been treated too badly by the white world to perceive it any differently.

The earlier coincidence of Mann's arriving at the Heartfields' is surpassed in remarkableness by a second even more improbable event. For, when Mann and a youthful black named Brinkley have been told to rescue a white woman and her two children if they can, the woman is Mrs. Heartfield. Although two such coincidences are deficiencies in realistic fiction, Wright even adds a third: when the Heartfields' house is reached, Mann climbs in through a window and resolves to kill Mrs. Heartfield and her two children, but the house tilts at the moment he is going to swing an axe. By this point, the reader is utterly flabbergasted. The story concludes with Mann's being shot for killing Mr. Heartfield. The problem is that sympathy for the oppressed does not function as the mortise and tenon joint in the plot structure.

But "Long Black Song," the third story in the collection, is almost as impressive as "Big Boy Leaves Home." Its pivotal point is the contrast between a preindustrial, rural, black folk culture and a rationalistic, industrial, white one. The former is reflected in the natural surroundings as the wife of the protagonist, Sarah, looks out over the land while the sun sets: "She saw green fields wrapped in the thickening gloam. It was as if they had left the earth, those fields, and were floating slowly skyward. The afterglow lingered, red, dying, somehow tenderly sad. And far away, in front of her, earth and sky met in a soft swoon of shadow. A cricket chirped, sharp and lonely; and it seemed she could hear it chirping long after it had stopped. Silas oughta c mon soon. Ahm tireda staying here by mahsef" (105). Sensitive to the rhythms of the natural world, Sarah gains satisfaction from the consequent harmony; but her husband, Silas, has gone to town and she is lonesome. Alone with her baby, she indulges in fantasies about the man she might have married, Tom, who is fighting in World War I: "Against the plush sky she saw a white bright day and a green cornfield and she saw Tom walking in his overalls and she was with Tom and he had his arm about her waist" (105). The paratactic syntax reflects her vision of the world: every part of it is equally valued, man's world and God's. But Silas has not quite fulfilled her as Tom did.

Into her world of natural rhythms and harmonies intrudes a car driven by a white man, a situation that Wright later developed into the white imperialist West violating black Africa in *Black Power*. When the white man, a door-to-door salesman of graphophones, asks Sarah why she allows her baby to beat on a clock with a stick, Wright's essential point becomes clear:

> "But why let her tear your clock up?"
> "It ain no good."
> "You could have it fixed."

"We ain got no money t be fixin' no clocks."
"Haven't you got a clock?"
"Naw."
"But how do you keep time?"
"We git erlong widout time."
"But how do you know when to get up in the morning?"
"We jus git up, thas all."
"But how do you know what time it is when you get up?"
"We gits up wid the sun."
"And at night, how do you tell when its night?"
"It gits dark when the sun goes down."
"Haven't you ever had a clock?"
She laughed and turned her face towards the silent fields. "Mistah, we don need no clock."
"Well, this beats everything! I don't see how in the world anybody can live without time."
"We just don need no time, Mistah." (108)

The white world equates time with money, but the black folk world equates it with natural values. But there is also a hint of seduction by white technology, a theme Wright later takes up again in "Man, God Ain't Like That . . . ," in that Sarah does enjoy the music produced by the graphophone. When she learns that the salesman is earning money in order to finance the study of science in college, her initial opinion that he is just a little boy receives confirmation. His definition of science—" 'why things are as they are' " (110)—is mere amusement to Sarah, whose earthiness precludes any metaphysical speculation, but it is a definition that contains within it a real conflict of much concern to Wright —the clash between a transcendental and a secular world-view, a clash he ultimately came to see as global in its implications.

In a recapitulation of Afro-American history, the salesman debauches Sarah. Wright suggests the sexual connotations of the banging sound of the baby's play by having the sound repeated after Sarah and the salesman have had sexual intercourse. Later the same night, when Silas returns, he is exulting in his good fortune: he has sold his cotton for $250, which will allow him to buy more land and retain a hired man; in other words, though he detests whites, he wants to emulate white economic values. Then Wright mars the story in a manner that recalls to the reader the improbabilities in "Down by the Riverside": for, when Silas finds no less than three clues that suggest he has been cuckolded (a straw hat, a yellow pencil, and a damp white handkerchief) Wright would have the reader believe that they had all been left in the bedroom by the graphophone salesman.

Although Silas wants to whip Sarah, the white world has clearly been responsible for the violation; for, just as in *Lawd Today* and in *Native Son*, the impingement of white power on black weaknesses causes violence to usurp love. Silas shoots and kills either the salesman or his companion (the reader never learns which), protectively tells Sarah to flee to safety, and waits pointlessly for the inevitable mob. After Sarah starts away with her child, she stops, watches the house, and remembers the peaceful, harmonious view of her world which is being irrevocably blemished by racial murder: "Somehow men, black men and white men, land and houses, green cornfields and grey skies, gladness and dreams, were all a part of that which made life good. Yes, somehow, they were linked, like the spokes in a spinning wheel. She felt they were. She knew they were. She felt it when she breathed and knew it when she looked. But she could not say how; she could not put her finger on it and when she thought hard about it it became all mixed up, like milk spilling suddenly. Or else it knotted in her throat . . ." (126). Her bittersweet reverie is interrupted by technology, by the blare of automobile horns that signal the oncoming white mob.

Wright's compulsive fire imagery presides in this third story's ending as Silas, after killing as many of the foe as possible, sits stoically in his house while it burns up. His widow, her world-view and life mutilated, runs "blindly across the fields, crying, 'Naw, Gawd!' " (128). Nihilism and despair are two of Wright's essential themes as is clear from the present-day impossibility of Sarah's pastoral vision and from Silas's despairing cry that " 'Yuh die ef yuh fight! Yuh die ef yuh don fight! Either way yuh die n it don mean nothin . . .' " (125).

Although the first three stories narrate the hopeless struggle of one black man against the racist mob, "Fire and Cloud," the fourth, is informed by the theme of collective resistance to white oppression; and this method seems to be the only realistic possibility if blacks are to be free. However, this penultimate story also raises an issue Wright never resolved: is race or class the primary cause of the social ills in America? Here he suggests, not convincingly, that Marxism can overcome racial injustice, although, as Harold Cruse has so cogently argued in *The Crisis of the Negro Intellectual*, race has always been more powerful as a social determinant in America than class. But, when Wright created "Fire and Cloud," he was a very idealistic Marxist.

The setting of "Fire and Cloud" is a southern town in the throes of the Depression. Blacks are starving because, as the bottom rungs on the economic ladder, they reap economic disaster even in the best of times. Nor can they use their agrarian skills to help themselves because white landowners have barred them from all the arable lands. In short, the milieu is rather heavy-handedly wrought by the author into a Marxist's delight that is ripe for social upheaval; but the protagonist, Reverend Dan Taylor, is a man who has always enjoyed good relations with the white community and has worked through it for his modest goals (such as stopping a lynching with the "beneficent" help of the Chief of Police). Reverend Taylor is in the difficult position of trying to get food for his starving brethren without irritating the white power structure while at the same time maintaining cordial relations with local Communists, whom he perceives to have the town's interests at heart.

Another of Wright's discomfiting coincidences, this one an adumbration of the incredible scene in *Native Son* in which Bigger is visited by all the important figures in his life, opens "Fire and Cloud." Reverend Taylor arrives home to find waiting for him the leaders of the white community; the whole of the Board of Deacons of Taylor's church which is led by a black Judas-informer, Deacon Smith; a black committee of ten that Taylor has earlier sent to City Hall to ask for food; and two Communists. Though a student of Naturalism, Wright felt so fettered by its stringencies that he had to flout it. His writing often shows an uncomfortable conflation of Realism and Symbolism—he here uses the two modes in an attempt to dramatize the three forces that are vying for Taylor's loyalty: the black community, the white power structure, and the Communists.

Taylor first goes to the church adjacent to his house in an unsuccessful attempt to placate the committee which has just returned from a fruitless attempt to get relief from City Hall. The minister offers them prayers, but they want food—and action. When he next goes into his house (where, because they have been put into different rooms, neither the white city leaders, the Communists, nor the Deacons realize anyone else is waiting), it is Hadley (a white man) and Green (black), the Communists, who take priority in Taylor's schedule. Hadley has rounded up some three thousand poor and hungry whites for a protest march to the City Hall but says that blacks will be difficult to summon without Reverend Taylor's name on the leaflets that the Communists want to distribute throughout the black community. But since Taylor has always worked *through* the white establishment, he is more than reluctant to lend his name to a Communist demonstration which will be declared illegal and which may well provoke violent reprisals from the capitalist power structure of the city. Though Hadley and Green argue persuasively—that if a great number of the 15,000 blacks in the community can be persuaded to march, their demands will have to be met, for they will be invincible in their numbers—Reverend Taylor still refuses to lend his name to what he fears will become war.

The next episode of Taylor with his visitors is particularly impressive. When he goes into his parlor where the powerful whites have been sequestered, he is greeted by the chief of police, by the head of the Industrial Squad (a euphemism for a gang of hoodlums who beat up Communists) and by the mayor, who calls Taylor "boy" and tells him to have a seat. They have learned of the imminent demonstration from the black traitor Deacon Smith, and of its Communist origins. Appealing to Taylor as a " 'good nigger' " and invoking loyalty to " 'good old Dixie,' " the three cajole the minister to lend his full strength to the task of cancelling the coming demonstration. The irony in the conversation is brutal when the Mayor inquires, " 'After all, we are human beings, aren't we?' " (148); and the suggestion of menace is unmistakable when he mentions that " 'It'll take a lot more than a summer cold to kill old warhorses like you and me, eh, Dan?' " (147). Though the chief of police and the head of the Industrial Squad confirm plainly the threat to Taylor's life that the mayor has only hinted at, Taylor refuses to block the demonstration that he knows may be the last resort of his hungry people.

The next white attempt to influence Taylor is, predictably,

violent: he is dragged into a car by a never-identified group of thugs, taken to the woods and whipped while being forced to say the Lord's Prayer in a sadistic parody of Christianity. Although Wright was implacably opposed to the other-worldliness of Christianity, he *was* willing nevertheless to entertain notions of a secular millennium; and the biblical ideas and imagery that inform this story suggest that eschatology is the possible result of the combining of Christianity and an atheistical political theory. With the whipping, Dan Taylor becomes a modern-day Moses; the biblical fire that led Moses and the Israelites in the night is transformed into the fiery pain in Taylor's back that leads him to the vision of the ultimate primacy that every black must invest in the collective good of his people. Staggering bloodied and aching through a white neighborhood in order to get home, Taylor sees a "new Heaven n . . . new Earth" that will be forged by a unification of the *people.* He is not certain that the Communists are correct that it will be a racially mixed proletariat that will emerge victorious, but he has had the Sign that his black race can be strong only through collective resistance. The Fire that leads him becomes, when he thinks of those who resist it, the flames of the Apocalypse: "Like a pillar of fire he went through the white neighborhood. Some days theys gonna burn! Some days theys gonna burn in Gawd Awmightys fire!" (167). And the fire also symbolizes the hellish life of black Americans: "Its *fire*! Like the fire that burned me las night! Its sufferin! Its hell! Ah cant bear this fire erlone!' " (178). Taylor, instructed by this fire, at last takes the mantle of leadership and gathers the black community which, joining with the poor whites, moves under the sun "like a pregnant cloud" (179)—the thousands-strong crowd, marching as one to demand food, has replaced the lone Taylor as the celestial guidance to the Promised Land.

Dan McCall, who has made the most insightful remarks about this story, points out that "the lessons of Southern history, and the lessons of Richard Wright's own previous work negate the lesson" of "Fire and Cloud."[9] The story's theme—that if blacks and poor whites will unite they can reach the Promised Land—gratifies any good Marxist; but it is unveiled wish-fulfillment. The inarticulate ending of the too-easy melding of blacks and whites in the quest of food underscores the fairy-tale nature of the piece.

"All the prose on the last two pages is bloated, throbbing with triumph at the expense of accuracy"; and the ending is a "*deus* (*Marxus*) *ex machina*."[10] Wright allowed visions of a Marxist Utopia to obscure his usually unrelentingly sharp eyes; and there is just the hint of realization of this when Taylor's eyes are finally described as "wet with tears, blurring his vision" (180).

The final story in the 1940 edition of *Uncle Tom's Children* is "Bright and Morning Star," which, like "Fire and Cloud" and unlike the other pieces in the book, has communism as a central focus. Sue, the protagonist, is an elderly but strong woman who, though she has had her fervent Christianity displaced by her sons' communism, has retained her common sense: she maintains a deep distrust of whites which, though inimical to the Marxist desire to racelessly unite the proletariat, is the only correct empirical response to the racial life of the deep South. Johnny-Boy, Sue's son, undaunted by his brother Sug's imprisonment for his work in the Communist party, is still avidly recruiting. Perhaps because he has never shared his mother's Christianity, he puts all his hopes and idealism into the party which he claims has taught him to see only rich and poor, not black or white. Reva (Revelation? Revolution?) is Johnny-Boy's white coworker and sweetheart. The other chief character in the story is a white Judas named Booker—in an obvious thrust at Booker T. Washington, who, by his accommodation to white precepts, betrayed black humanistic values.

Early in the story, when Reva tells Sue that the sheriff has somehow learned there is to be a secret party meeting at the home of Reva's father, Sue decides that a white spy must have infiltrated the group and that it must be up to Johnny-Boy to contact all the members and to call off the meeting. He has scarcely left on the mission when the sheriff and his men break into Sue's home to learn his whereabouts. Although she is heroic in her refusal to disclose where he is or what he is doing, Sue is beaten for it and left so weak that she becomes, momentarily and uncharacteristically, a foil for white plotting.

When Booker, whom Sue already suspects as being the informer, arrives at the house soon thereafter, telling her that Johnny-Boy has been captured by the sheriff and his men before he was able to sound the alarm to tell the party members, the words "Jesus hep me" (199) crowd the battered Sue's brain; but she nonetheless makes the appalling mistake of giving him the names. She quickly realizes her mistake, takes a shortcut to Foley's Woods, where Johnny-Boy is being tortured, and kills Booker with the pistol she has hidden under the winding-sheet the sheriff and his men assume she has brought to cover her soon-to-be-dead son, thus ensuring that the membership list of the cell is kept from those who would destroy the movement. So, like "Fire and Cloud" and unlike the other three short stories that stress individual response to oppression, "Bright and Morning Star" does end with a measure of triumph: despite the fact that both Johnny-Boy and Sue are murdered by the sheriff's men in circumstances that would place the story squarely in the tradition of the first three in the anthology, there is the chance that, since the list is safe, the Communist party will be able to survive and grow; but unlike "Fire and Cloud," the stirring deed is the action of an individual, not of a group.

Despite its emphasis on individual action the piece is unmistakably Socialist Realism, however, and, as such, it is marred by the deficiencies in plotting that seem trademarks of Wright's efforts in that literary style. Sue's blurting out the list to a white man she suspects is unconvincing to say the least; the likelihood in 1938 or even now that a black man and a white girl would fall in love and unite to fight under a Marxist banner and in the deep South was, and is, extremely unlikely. But the young Wright is so enamored of his vision of the Holy Grail a la Lenin and Marx that he betrays his own experience. He is trying hard to perceive social reality as Johnny-Boy did, as poor versus rich, not black versus white, but Wright's empirical observations peep insistently from behind his Marxist theorizing—the smooth-talking Booker's perfidy causes the deaths of Johnny-Boy and Sue; and Sue is all too justified in her regarding most whites as monsters. She is also sadly right that it is just as well for the sweet Reva that Johnny-boy will be killed, for their love for each other is utterly impossible. Though the young Wright was trying hard to perceive social reality in the way the party dictated that he and Johnny-Boy see it, his experiences caused him to create Sue, and to focus his sympathies on her.

The four short stories that comprise the 1938 edition of *Uncle*

Tom's Children are arranged according to a principle of organization that is marred by the 1940 edition's inclusion at its beginning of "The Ethics of Living Jim Crow," which, as an autobiographical vignette, would fit uneasily in *any* anthology of short stories, and "Bright and Morning Star" at the end; for, as the reader has seen, it is a strange conflation of individual action and collectivist apocalypse that is unlike any of the other selections.[11] The stories in the original collection—"Big Boy Leaves Home," "Down by the Riverside," "Long Black Song," and "Fire and Cloud"—demonstrate an authorial emphasis that shifts from black people combating white oppression as individuals (Big Boy, Mann, and Silas) to a culmination of militant, collectivist black action in "Fire and Cloud." But, as they shift in emphasis, the less convincing they become as the movement from individual to mass protest is developed. "Big Boy Leaves Home" rings truer than "Fire and Cloud" because the latter is Marxist tract but the former is a powerful recreation of southern myth. Wright, the extreme individualist, may have *intended* to celebrate the glory of Marx's collectivist proletariat, but what he *achieved* was a diminution of his audience's attention because of the shrill, propagandistic nature of his message. "Big Boy Leaves Home" emerges as the finest piece in the collection and also as one of Wright's best efforts, along with *Native Son*, *Black Boy*, and "The Man Who Lived Underground."

CHAPTER 3

His Fulfillment

THE publication of *Native Son* in 1940 was the beginning of a black literature that refused to compromise with many white expectations. In Bigger Thomas, Wright created a monster, but one who was the inevitable product of America. As such, he is a brutalized, stunted creature who deludes himself into thinking two gruesome murders are the means by which he will be redeemed. He is not a hero (although some critics have tried to argue that he is) but a "nigger"; but the *cause* for his debasement, his lack of identity with humanity, is white society. Bigger is America's native son, the heritage of white racism. The name "Bigger Thomas" is itself suggestive, and Wright's custom is often to use names descriptively. Bigger is a "bigger nigger" who is worse than Uncle Tom, his prototype in the sense that Bigger is more enslaved by the hopeless assumptions of black inferiority than Harriet Beecher Stowe's stereotype is. In accepting himself as a brutalized, deformed man, Bigger confirms the implications of his name.

And the other characters in the story—some of whom accept Bigger as just the animal he is; some who blindly avert their eyes from the truth—all sadly live up to the expectations the reader develops about them. It eventually seems that they are all playing parts in a dramatized psychology book, but the "title" of that book is not immediately clear without considering the literary contributions about blackness in America by that other towering but later figure in black literature, Eldridge Cleaver. In *Soul on Ice*, Cleaver contrives a myth to dramatize the sexual basis of white racism. The major figures in his myth are the Omnipotent Administrator, the Supermasculine Menial, the Ultrafeminine, and the Amazon. The Omnipotent Administrator is the white man in a position of power, who, alienated from the Body, has an overdeveloped Mind. His black counterpart, the Supermasculine Menial, by contrast, is estranged from the Mind; but, having an overdeveloped body, he, as man as doer, performs a Brute Power Function and serves as a "walking phallus symbol."[1]

The Omnipotent Administrator's bride, the Ultrafeminine, is described by Cleaver's old fat Lazarus: " 'I love her skin, her soft, smooth white skin. I like to just lick her white skin as if sweet, fresh honey flows from her pores, and just to touch her long, soft, silky hair. There's a softness about a white woman, something delicate and soft inside her. But a nigger bitch seems to be full of steel, granite-hard and resisting, not soft and submissive like a white woman' " (148). The end of the description is also a definition of the Amazon, the bride of the Supermasculine Menial. The crucial distinction between the two female figures in Cleaver's myth is that the Amazon is a symbol of slavery; the Ultrafeminine, of freedom. The Omnipotent Administrator, a white, has told the Supermasculine Menial, a black, "men die for freedom, but black men die for white women, who are the symbols of freedom" (149).

With this theory Cleaver has given his reader the means of understanding the sexual dynamics of *Native Son*, a novel he himself admires, and indeed, of most of Wright's works. In *Native Son*, Buckley, Bigger's prosecutor, corresponds to the Omnipotent Administrator; Mary Dalton, to the Ultrafeminine; Bessie Mears, to the Amazon; and, of course, Bigger, to the Supermasculine Menial. The classification does not exhaust the possibilities (Mr. Dalton could be, for instance, another example of the Administrator; Mrs. Thomas, of the Amazon), but it does establish the major representatives of each mythical figure. These mythical roles add to the dimensions of each character in *Native Son* and to virtually every other character in every other work of Wright's; for he presents over and over again the theme that the Supermasculine Menial, impotent to die for anything as ennobling as Freedom, must lower his sights to mere symbol and lose his life because of the questionably worthwhile white woman.

I *The Narrative*

In *Native Son*, a novel that is quintessentially Wrightian, the dedication and the epigraph are also characteristic of him. His first published novel is dedicated to his mother, who taught him "to revere the fanciful and the imaginative." Even before reading the book, then, the reader has an indication that Wright's Naturalism and Realism are leavened with symbol and myth; for he signals that he was much more willing to rely on figurative language than were other Naturalists like Frank Norris or Theodore Dreiser. The epigraph is from Job, the source of many of Wright's inscriptions, since Bigger is like Job in that he has done nothing to justify his brutalization.

The first scene depicts the brutal killing of a rat. Bigger's day begins, and will end, in bloodshed. When Bigger crushes the rat's head with a shoe, Wright offers the reader a resonant, prospective irony, for this act anticipates the manner of his girlfriend's death. Bigger always destroys the heads of his victims because it is in the mind that the causes of his exclusion lie. The rat's blood is covered with a newspaper: bloodstain imagery animates the entire narrative as an implication that violence predominates in black experience.

The opening violence includes not only the killing of an animal but also the emotional violence generated by the four members of the Thomas family against one another. Since they live in only one room, they inevitably have no privacy, no way to conceal personal anxieties. As a matrifocal unit, the family revolves around Mrs. Thomas; and Bigger directs much of his intense hatred toward her because she functions as a representative of the oppressions in his life. One example of her attempts to tyrannize Bigger is her cruel musing to him, her oldest son, that she sometimes wonders why she gave birth to him. This heartless, unanswerable question directed to the necessarily innocent offspring amounts to rejection of him and links itself to society's similar rejection of him that leads Bigger into a kind of emotional free-fall. Her predictions that he will end on the gallows will be fulfilled, and she will unknowingly be one of the causes. She further oppresses him when she insists on personally defining "manhood" for him—Bigger's manhood and the question of what manhood is lie at the center of *Native Son*. She wants him to be a "man," but that to her means he should be a chauffeur for a white family named Dalton. Bigger is dubious and apprehensive of the rubric into which she wishes to thrust him, partly because he wonders how she can urge him to be a man when she has had negligible control over her own life and when her attempts at self-definition have been so pitiful.

Her response to the family's nightmarish nonexistence is to abandon hope for any fulfillment in this life, but she is convinced that the next will compensate. To Bigger and his creator, otherworldliness is futile because it precludes efforts at reorienting one's self, at causing a secular redemption. When other black characters in the novel turn to various diversions for salvation—Mrs. Thomas, to religion; Bessie, to alcohol—there is no indication that such responses really result in the alleviation of quotidian distress; they are all escapist. Only Green, Bigger's predecessor at the Daltons', may be able to use his escapism to some small end in the changing of his conditions, for he rests his hopes of salvation in education.

Bigger, the most pitiful of the black crew, is not an escapist—he feels too closed in for even that small flight of fancy. As he leaves his apartment, he sees a large poster of Buckley, who is later to become his prosecutor but who is now running again for State's Attorney: "He looked at the poster: the white face was fleshy but stern: one hand was uplifted and its index finger pointed straight out into the street at each passer-by."[2] The poster says, "IF YOU BREAK THE LAW, YOU CAN'T WIN!"—but Bigger loses whether he breaks the law or not.

He is apprehensive about his late-afternoon interview at the Daltons' and spends a shiftless, temporizing day preparing for it. When he runs into one of his poolroom cronies, Gus, with whom he has previously agreed that their gang will commit a robbery for some quick cash, he now feels listless, uncertain that the robbery is a good idea. When the two young blacks notice a plane flying overhead, Bigger voices the wistful, impossible desire to fly himself—this desire is just one more indication of his figurative imprisonment before he is literally jailed. Bigger's dreams will never be realized because whites do not allow blacks to do or to be anything, and the word "nothing" is used frequently throughout the narrative as a denial of the existence of anything positive in the lives of the oppressed. Bigger says, " 'Goddammit, look! We live here and they live there. We black and they white. They got things and we don't. They do things and we can't. It's just like living in jail. Half the time I feel like I'm on the outside of the world peeping in through a knot-hole in the fence' " (23). The profound sense of exclusion from America is the keynote of Bigger's life and death.

To pass the time until the robbery of Blum's, Bigger and the member of the gang he is closest to, Jack, go to a double-feature movie: "The Regal was just opening. Bigger lingered in the lobby and looked at the colored posters while Jack bought the tickets. Two features were advertised: one, *The Gay Woman*, was pictured on the posters in images of white men and women lolling on beaches, swimming, and dancing in night clubs; the other, *Trader Horn*, was shown on the posters in terms of black men and black women dancing against a wild background of barbaric jungle" (32). *The Gay Woman* blinds Bigger to the truth about white America and his own racial heritage, for it creates in him the impression that all whites are rich, pampered, indulged capitalists. As for the impression made by *Trader Horn*, it reinforces the stereotypical image of black Africa as a locus of savagery. Chicago is the real barbaric jungle, but Bigger is so ignorant about his racial past and about the true nature of American society that he automatically accepts both films as accurate.

The movie ended, the dismaying prospect of his 5:30 interview with the white family still looming large, Bigger feels disoriented and apprehensive. He reacts by letting his mind play morbidly on the robbery of Blum's: it would be not only their largest to date but also, dismayingly, their first of a white man. He finds himself incapable of action, and, at his poolroom hangout only a few doors from Blum's, he starts a noisy row with his cronies in which he humiliates Gus and calls so much attention to his gang that the robbery is impossible. He shuffles dazedly home to muse about the aborted robbery and to keep his mind obstinately turned away from what has obsessed him all day.

When the time for the appointment at last arrives, the interview at 4605 Drexel Boulevard, the Daltons', forces Bigger to acknowledge how totally deluded he is about the white world: "He had not expected anything like this; he had not thought that this world would be so utterly different from his own that it would intimidate him" (47). What converges at this interview are two historical currents symbolized by 4605 Drexel Boulevard and 3721 Indiana Avenue, Bigger's address; for the former is the home of a wealthy white liberal whose position is maintained by the exploitation of the poor and uneducated; and 3721 Indiana is one example of this proletariat. In fact, Wright even makes Mr. Dalton Bigger's landlord.

The question that arises concerns who is more deluded about the other, Bigger or his prospective employer; for, when Mr. Dalton tells Bigger, " 'I was a boy myself once and I think I know how things are. So just be yourself' " (51), it is despairingly clear he has absolutely no idea " 'how things are.' " But his new chauffeur will indeed be himself—stunted, brutalized, unregenerated. Perhaps the only moment of humor in this otherwise unrelievedly grim narrative occurs in the same interview when Mr. Dalton asks Bigger if he would steal if he had a job, for Bigger's response is, of course, that he does not steal. Like the white woman in *Black Boy* who asked the young Wright the same question, Mr. Dalton unknowingly assumes Bigger is either naive or stupid enough to answer it honestly. The most powerful piece of dramatic irony in the novel appears when Mr. Dalton says, " 'I don't think we'll have any trouble' " (52), for he suffers later the killing, decapitation, and burning of his daughter. This crime is America's heritage of racism; and Wright is warning America that its policy of racial exclusion has created a monster that may destroy it.

Though the larger, symbolic aspects of Bigger that so unnerve the reader elude Mr. Dalton, he does consider him a sign, a representation, of blackness. Like Mr. Norton, the northern liberal in *Invisible Man*, Mr. Dalton feels that, by funneling charitable monies into the black community, he is helping alleviate racial problems. He expects Bigger to be impressed that he supports Bigger's "people" through contributions to the National Association for the Advancement of Colored People. Bigger is puzzled: he does not think of himself primarily as simply a specimen of blackness, but as an individual who is different from other people, black or white. Further evidence that Mr. Dalton's condescendingly ingratiating information has missed its mark is the fact that Bigger has never heard of the association. Bigger has no individual identity in the house. Even Peggy, the Daltons' cook, thinks of the new chauffeur as an example of blackness rather than as an individual.

Bigger gets an unusual sense of pleasure from driving the Daltons' car: "He had a keen sense of power when driving; the feel of a car added something to him. He loved to press his foot against the pedal and sail along watching others stand still, seeing the asphalt road unwind under him" (63). Denied freedom of physical movement in his cramped environment, denied any kind of mobility in society, he now keenly enjoys physical movement—and he can indulge temporarily in illusions of freedom. When his first duty is to take Mary, the Daltons' daughter, to the university, the task culminates in the ironic fulfillment of one of Bigger's daydreams about what his new job would be like. Before his appointment at the Daltons', he has imagined that "Mr. Dalton was a millionaire. Maybe he had a daughter who was a hot kind of a girl: maybe she spent lots of money; maybe she'd like to come to the South Side and see the sights sometimes. Or maybe she had a secret sweetheart and only he would know about it because he would have to drive her around; maybe she would give him money not to tell" (36).

Most of his fantasies prove perversely to be true, although not at all in the way Bigger has anticipated. Instead of going to school, Mary instructs her chauffeur to drive her to 16 Lake Street, the headquarters of the Communist party in Chicago. She causes him to feel extremely uncomfortable and anxious because "she responded to him as if he were human" (66). Wright links this scene with the final consequences of it: Mary tells her driver, who is confused by her adamant alteration of the orders he received, that he will understand " 'better bye and bye' " (66). When Bigger is in jail, the Reverend Hammond tells him, " 'Son, there's a place where we can be together again in the great bye and bye' " (278). The preacher's ignorant echo of Mary's foolish words serves to link the two scenes together and also to underscore Wright's disgust at otherworldliness.

Soon after Mary's foolish words, her Communist boyfriend, Jan Erlone, who is probably modeled on Jan Wittenberger, who *alone* treated Wright as an individual rather than as a social statistic in Wright's John Reed Club days, joins them. Insisting that Bigger sit between them, Jan drives: "There were white people to either side of him; he was sitting between two vast looming walls. Never in his life had he been so close to a white woman" (68). Since they seem to think of blacks as exotic primitives, Jan and Mary, like the whites who went slumming in Harlem during the 1920s, ask Bigger to take them to " 'a *real* place' "—to a place that will meet their romantic fantasies about black life. The couple are phony hipsters: they want to be black for a few hours on Saturday night— and then return, after their fling, to the security of the Communist sanctuary or of the moneyed home.

When Bigger takes them to Ernie's Kitchen Shack, he takes them to a restaurant modeled after a real one but with its name slightly changed.[3] In fact, Wright stays so close to the real world that the charge that *Native Son* exaggerates is completely wrong-headed; in fact, the book is understated. Jan and Mary play black, just as Bigger and Gus had played white:

> The waitress brought beer and chicken.
> "This is simply grand!" Mary exclaimed.
> "You've got something there," Jan said, looking at Bigger. "Did I say that right, Bigger?"
> Bigger hesitated.
> "That's the way they say it," he spoke flatly. (73)

As Saturday-night Bohemians, Jan and Mary regard blacks as James Fenimore Cooper regarded the American Indians—as extensions of their egotistical fantasies. They, like Mr. Dalton and the cook, do not view Bigger as an individual. They are as ignorant of what he is as he is of what they are; and all three of them are woefully unconscious that, because of the crushing ignorance on all sides, Bigger is about to kill. They are simply interested in him as an example of an oppressed minority and as a potential member of the Communist party.

In order to recruit Bigger, Jan tries to establish the party's credentials with blacks by mentioning the Scottsboro boys, nine black youths wrongfully indicted on charges of having raped two white women in 1931; and at this point in the narrative the book's most severe philosophical weakness appears. The novel first hintingly supports that the horrors of racism might be alleviated by the union of blacks with poor and downtrodden whites; yet ultimately, in disclosing the truly unregenerate nature of Bigger's debasement, *Native Son* engenders doubt that any "mere" proletarian solidarity could mitigate the horrors that are all too frequently the concomitants of dark complexions. Because Wright himself was not sure whether class or race was *the* determining factor in society, the novel inevitably reflects his confusion. If racism is dominant over economic realities, then such a union of poor white people and black people would not remove racial prejudice. If, on the other hand, the Marxist theory that all social phenomena follow from economic privations is true, then that union would be a necessary one for blacks and impoverished whites.

The three young people consume a good deal of beer and rum—so much, in fact, that, by the time Bigger drives the couple back to Drexel Boulevard Mary is drunk. After Jan leaves, Bigger almost has to carry Mary to her bedroom and put her to bed. When blind Mrs. Dalton comes into the bedroom to check on her daughter, Bigger becomes terrified. He knows automatically that, if a black man is discovered in a white woman's bedroom, there is only one conclusion whites will draw. In an effort to keep Mary from making any noise that would alarm her mother, he accidently smothers her with a pillow—and ensures his own death. Ironically, although he does not rape Mary, he considers it; and he is convicted for the murder *and* rape of her, although the charge of rape cannot possibly be substantiated, since her body was burned. Eldridge Cleaver's myth of "types," white and black, explains cogently why the bedroom scene is inevitably fatal for Bigger: in the assumed violation of her, he rapes America itself, at least in the subconscious labyrinth of racist white psyches.

As one of Wright's underground men, Bigger takes Mary's corpse to the Daltons' basement in order to burn it in the furnace. The atmosphere is weirdly Gothic—a dark basement with flames casting diabolical shadows—and Wright's debt to Edgar Allan Poe and Nathaniel Hawthorne seems indubitable. The horror builds, and the most brutal part of the scene comes as a decapitation. Since the furnace will not accommodate Mary's whole body, Bigger beheads it: "Gently, he sawed the blade into the flesh [of the neck] and struck a bone" (90). Not being able to cut off the head with a knife, he finds a hatchet and uses it to sever the head: "Quickly, he wrapped the head of the body in the newspapers and used the wad to push the bloody trunk of the body deeper into the furnace" (91). Then he turns on an exhaust fan so that the stench of Mary's burning flesh will not indicate his crime. And yet, even after all this brutality the reader still sympathizes with the man who was driven by his environment to commit such a sensationally gruesome crime.

Book Two, "Flight," which opens the next Sunday morning, presents Bigger's deluding himself into a millennialist trance over the meaning of his crime: "He had murdered and had created new life for himself" (101). He does not realize the moral contradiction in the assertion that in murder lies resurrection, nor does he know his sense of elation is at any rate temporary because he will soon be arrested and executed. "Though he had killed by accident, not once did he feel the need to tell himself that it had been an accident. . . . In a certain sense he knew that the girl's death had not been accidental. He had killed many times before, only on those other times there had been no handy victim or circumstance to make visible or dramatic his will to kill" (101). Thus he intentionally deludes himself into thinking the killing of Mary Dalton was premeditated; for, had he admitted it was a Pavlovian response to a hostile environment, he would have had to acknowledge that it had no significance other than as an indication that his responses were controlled by his fear of the whites. He wants no part of honesty at this point: "Like a man reborn, he wanted to test and taste each thing now to see how it went; like a man risen up from a long illness, he felt deep and wayward whims" (106). There are times, though, when he is more candid with himself: "He had acted too hastily and accidentally" (123).

What *is* true about the first killing is that, for once, a black is directing violence toward a white rather than having it directed by the white toward him, as is usually the case; for once, a black person is acting rather than passively existing; and, for once, the first time in his whole life, Bigger has felt self-esteem. This feeling or reaction was brought about through an act of violence, for all other normal roads to the ego were blocked to him, a black. The heart of Wright's accusation of America is, therefore, that the only way Bigger can feel he is a man is by the destruction of other people. If the victim is a relatively innocent one, as was Mary Dalton, it makes no difference to Bigger, for at this point all whites are alike to him.

Most of the rest of Book Two is concerned with solving the crime and with apprehending the criminal. Wright has stated the reason the crime was not solved immediately: "If there had been *one* person in the Dalton household who viewed Bigger Thomas as a human being, the crime would have been solved in half an hour.

Did not Bigger himself know that it was the denial of his personality that enabled him to escape detection for so long?"[4] In fact, the crime could have remained forever unsolved if the furnace, which saved Bigger from detection earlier by "eating" his prey, had not given him away: it has grown so cold in the Daltons' basement, where Britten, the Daltons' private investigator, and the newspaper reporters have gathered, that Bigger tries to clean out the ashes in the furnace to make a better fire. The crime is then discovered, significantly, by a newspaper reporter; for the use of newspaper headlines, which are often luridly sensational and inflammatory, is prominent in *Native Son*, and their function is similar to that in Wright's earlier "Hearst Headline Blues." The reporter solves the murder case by forcing Bigger out of the way and by shoveling the ashes out of the furnace himself, discovering one of Mary's earrings and some of her bones. Bigger runs for his life, and he is following the pattern of flight that Wright was obsessed by in "Big Boy Leaves Home," *The Outsider*, and *Black Boy*.

In flight, Bigger's previous self-deception about psychological redemption is forced to the surface of his mind: "this whole vague white world which could do things this quickly was more than a match for him . . . soon it would track him down and have it out with him" (221). Bigger's rebirth through violence is not only delusory, it is extremely evanescent. Thus *Native Son* is not about black redemption as some critics have argued, because Bigger acts only out of selfish motives (and in this respect he is again the inevitable product of American society), as his slaying of the meek and mild Bessie, his "girlfriend," indicates. He murders her because she knows he killed Mary Dalton. Her murder is rendered as one of the most crudely violent episodes in American fiction. Ironically, he *does* rape Bessie, who has been until this time his willing sexual partner but who is now too frightened by his admission of murder to be receptive to him. In the rape he is perhaps allotting himself a bit of bestial pleasure which he never seriously sought with Mary Dalton but which he knows he will be convicted for "enjoying." Then, as Bessie sleeps, he smashes her head with a brick:

He took a deep breath and his hand gripped the brick and shot upward and paused a second and then plunged downward through the darkness to the accompaniment of a deep short grunt from his chest and landed with a thud. *Yes*! There was a dull gasp of surprise, then a moan. No, that must not be! He lifted the brick again and again, until in falling it struck a sodden mass that gave softly but stoutly to each landing blow. Soon he seemed to be striking a wet wad of cotton, of some damp substance whose only life was the jarring of the brick's impact. He stopped, hearing his own breath heaving in and out of his chest. He was wet all over, and cold. How many times he had lifted the brick and brought it down he did not know. All he knew was that the room was quiet and that the job was done. (222)

Obviously Bessie is dead, but at the trial it is asserted she did not die until after she had tried to crawl out of the air shaft in which he had dumped her body; but this assertion might be either an inconsistency in the novel or a lie at the trial. Or perhaps it is best interpreted symbolically: Bigger cannot kill the "symbol of his Negro personality"[5]—Bessie has been as meek, cringing, and submissive as Bigger has been around the Dalton family. Moreover, her surname, Mears, a homophone of both "mere" and "mirrors," underscores this interpretation.

A massive police force is scouring the ghetto for Bigger; he is promptly caught, and Book Three, "Fate," opens with Bigger in his cell. He realizes he has been self-deceived, blind. And, just as there was somewhere a murderous instinct in him to eradicate white blindness through Mary's murder, he finds himself once again in the presence of sightlessness, and he reacts with thoughts about the annihilation of it: "He had reached out and killed and had not solved anything, so why not reach inward and kill that which had duped him?" (255). But he has a beast's instinct to live.

After Bigger realizes his blindness, most of the people in his life crowd around him in his prison cell. Of course, this long scene with all the central characters crowded together is an impossibility, but it allows Wright, the artist, to dramatize his protagonist's relationship with society in a telling manner. Bigger has long since rejected the otherworldly orientation of his mother's preacher, Reverend Hammond; but Jan Erlone represents something quite different when he visits the killer of his girlfriend: human understanding. Jan recognizes the value of Bigger's hatred: " 'It's your right to hate me, Bigger. I see now that you couldn't do anything else but that it was all you had' " (267). "For the first time in his [Bigger's] life a white man had become a human being . . ." (268). Boris Max, mentioned early in the novel (76), does not appear until this scene in Bigger's cell. Although it is not clear whether he himself is a Communist or not, he undertakes Bigger's defense because Buckley is dragging the name of the Communist party into the case and because Buckley helped to create men like Bigger. Bigger has one other visitor to his cell that most readers of *Native Son* seem to overlook in their exegeses: the black "lunatic" temporarily placed in Bigger's cell is one of the few morally sane men in the book. He shouts, " 'I'll tell 'im [the President] you make us live in such crowded conditions in the South Side that one out of every ten of us is insane!' " (318).

Eventually the Daltons, Bigger's gang, and his family visit him in prison. The scene with his family, one of the few in the book that evinces any positive emotion, qualifies James Baldwin's contention in "Many Thousands Gone" that Bigger is cut off from the black community:

> He had lived and acted on the assumption that he was alone, and now he saw he had not been. What he had done made others suffer. No matter how much he would long for them to forget him, they would not be able to. His family was a part of him, not only in blood, but in spirit. He sat on the cot and his mother knelt at his feet. Her face was lifted to his; her eyes were empty, eyes that looked upward when the last hope of earth had failed. (277)

Bigger was excluded from the larger opportunities of America but not totally from the black community. It is true that it is difficult for Bigger to respond warmly to his mother, but that is because she believes in another world while her son is as militantly secular as Wright. Bigger believes that "when he died, it would be over, forever" (278).

With the tentative rapprochement between Bigger and his mother; with his dual recognitions, humanistically allied to each other, that whites *may* be human; and that he is *not* rootless and beholden only to himself but a part, if only in memory, of the black community, Bigger has achieved some measure of vision; and the story of Bigger Thomas virtually ends. All that is left for him, for the judge, and for the reader is to ponder his fate—and whether he deserves it.

II *Assessments of the Novel's Conclusion*

Much of the conclusion of *Native Son* is concerned with Max's attempt to give his client some self-understanding and a broader perspective. The problem here is that Max's Marxist visions explain class but not racial conflict; and, since race has been more important than class as a social determinant in America, Wright's use of Marx invites the charge of wish-fulfillment. Bigger is honest with Max about the first killing. " 'But Bigger, when Mrs. Dalton came into the room, why didn't you stop right there and tell her what was wrong? You wouldn't 've been in all this trouble then. . . .' 'Mr. Max, so help me God, I couldn't do nothing when I turned around and saw that woman coming to that bed. Honest to God, I didn't know what I was doing . . .' " (325). Bigger's actions are completely determined by the environment. What he received from killing the two women, as he tells Max, was a temporary feeling of freedom. Bigger wants a secular redemption, but he is nothing. His options are closed; he is going to die. The only decision he has left to make is whether he will die in hope or in hatred.

When his trial begins, he is led to court through "an underground tunnel" (339); for Wright persistently literalizes his metaphors. Bigger, an underground man, has always been in a prison called the South Side of Chicago, and Wright makes the underground and prison actual as well as iconic. At the trial itself, Max's basic argument to the judge (there is no jury) is that being black in America is a radically extenuating circumstance. Relative to Max's speech, which is eighteen pages long in the Harper Perennial Classic edition, Wright admitted that Book Three was written to allow him to express his own opinions (*Quest*, 173). Since Max is the thinnest of disguises for the author himself, Wright can explain in Book Three what he has already dramatized in Book One and Book Two.

After acknowledging the instinctive nature of the first killing, Max-Wright explains why the defendant was so eager to convince himself that it was premeditated: " 'But, after he murdered, he accepted the crime. And that's the important thing. It was the first full act of his life; it was the most meaningful, exciting and stirring thing that had ever happened to him. He accepted it because it made him free, gave him the possibility of choice, of action, the opportunity to act and to feel that his actions carried weight' " (364). This statement expresses the meaning of the history of Bigger Thomas and 12 million other people (which was the black population in 1940): *nothing*. To transcend the emptiness of black history, some black men have turned inevitably to the only secular avenue available—violence.

Max then continues his defense with a most perplexing statement: " 'The actions that resulted in the death of those two women were as instinctive and inevitable as breathing or blinking one's eyes. It [*sic*] was an act of creation!' " (366). Apparently the antecedent for the pronoun "it" is the first killing, but the crucial point is how can murder be "creative"? Since Mary's death results in Bigger's imprisonment, trial, and execution, the assertion seems to have more a mystical, emotive value than a literal import. But at the conclusion of *Native Son*, Max seems to reject the notion of murder as creation when he accurately interprets the significance of Bigger: " 'Your Honor, is this boy alone in feeling deprived and baffled? Is he an exception? Or are there others? There are others, Your Honor, millions of others, Negro and white, and that is what makes our future seem a looming image of violence' " (368). Bigger represents modern man—one deprived, excluded, dislocated; and what makes him so frightening is that he is in every man, although he is not *all* of every man.

Moreover, Bigger's life meant no less than the lives of most Americans, as Wright knew: "Most of us 20th century Americans are reluctant to admit the tragically low quality of experience of the broad American masses; feverish radio programs, super advertisements, streamlined sky scrapers, million-dollar movies, and mass productions have somehow created the illusion in us that we are 'rich' in our emotional lives."[6] Bigger's life was thin because American life, and all human life, Wright eventually felt, is nugatory. Many of the bourgeois diversions (expensive cars, clothes, food) Bigger was excluded from were meretricious; but he had no way of knowing that, and such knowledge could be of no comfort to him anyway. He was "empty of human values because American culture was empty of human values. He was a monster. But he was also human."[7]

As Bigger awaits death, he is torn between nihilism and the possibility that his life has had value: "He wanted to be free of everything that stood between him and his end, him and the full and terrible realization that life was over without meaning, without anything being settled, without conflicting impulses being resolved" (382). Although Max tries to console Bigger with a vision of change through Marxism, this view underplays race in favor of social class and is, for that reason, instinctively odd-sounding to the black man. When Bigger goes to the electric chair, he is a man who is utterly determined to convince himself that what he has done has had value:

> "I didn't want to kill!" Bigger shouted. "But what I killed for, I *am*! It must've been pretty deep in me to make me kill! I must have felt it awful hard to murder. . . ."
>
> Max lifted his hand to touch Bigger, but did not.
>
> "No; no; no. . . . Bigger, not that. . . ." Max pleaded despairingly.
>
> "What I killed for must've been good!" Bigger's voice was full of frenzied anguish. "It must've been good! When a man kills, it's for something. . . . I didn't know I was really alive in this world until I felt things hard enough to kill for 'em. . . . It's the truth, Mr. Max. I can say it now, 'cause I'm going to die. I know what I'm saying real good and I know how it sounds. But I'm all right. I feel all right when I look at it that way. . . ." (391-92)

Max leaves, groping "for his hat like a blind man" (392). During the summation Max appears to understand not only his client's social existence, but his individuality. But, coming into Bigger's cell as he is about to be executed, the murderer becomes to Max a mystery as he tries to account for his feelings that the crimes are in some way virtuous.[8] Disoriented by Bigger's proto-Existentialist affirmation and emotionally involved with him enough to hope Bigger can become one with himself before his death, Max is disappointed that Bigger will not substitute his individualist world-view for a Marxist vision. Whereas Max feels that Bigger could find serenity by accepting the fact that he is largely a result of a horribly racist environment, Bigger, like many critics and readers of the book, cannot accept that he is merely such a by-product. It is as a social statistic, then, that Bigger is comprehensible to Max: but, as an individual, he is too nightmarish a figure for his lawyer to accept. Max cannot understand Bigger's deep personal desire to justify the two killings; he cannot see that the only way Bigger can feel what he is, is through killing. In a sense, it is Bigger's pulsing and essential humanness that is his problem, not his beastliness; for he did what most men in the same circumstances would have done—and that is "the tragedy of modern man, that he can attain autonomy only by destruction and eventual self-destruction."[9]

Max, in his confusion, echoes the reader's shock at Bigger's abrupt, seemingly bizarre affirmation. One reason that this terminal, frenzied moral acceptance of the worth of Bigger's deeds is so jarring is that Wright has acted throughout the book as if he were a thoroughgoing environmentalist before veering toward value judgment in the last couple of pages. If all social action is inevitable, then Bigger cannot emerge victorious over what he has had no choice about—and the question of victory does not obtain. But the reader finds the question in his mind in spite of himself. Bigger kills Mary Dalton because of *uncontrollable* fear of being discovered in her bedroom by Mrs. Dalton; and he premeditates Bessie's murder because he cannot deal in any other way with the fear that she may inform on him. Because of his instinct for survival, he has no choice *but* to kill. But the book in its final pages becomes a rough fusion between Naturalist determinism and the demand for Bigger's observers to respond normatively to him, his crimes, his affirmation. Max's "groping blindness" epitomizes every reader's initial dilemma and forecasts varied interpretations of the conclusion.

The reader feels, as the book ends, that he may have been led down the garden path by the author. If he has expected Dreiser-like inevitability, the reader finds himself faced instead with a situation that appears to demand sophisticated moral inference. It is undeniable that the book suffers from a change of tone in the last few pages, but the reader comes to believe it *can* ultimately be construed consistently, environmentally. An objective second look at the closing scene reveals that the significance of Bigger's life is that he is so oppressed that he considers killing an act of creation; he embraces the reversal of human values that his murders entail, but he does not transcend it, nor does he allow it to be applied to him; he is descendentalized man.

Bigger dies trying to convince himself that his murders are good. He cannot accept that he is nothing; his life can have no meaning because of the conditions of his existence; and, as a result, he does a very human thing: he tries to convince himself that the perversion of murder is morally healthy. His tragedy is that, in order to feel any self-esteem whatsoever, he must completely reject traditional moral values because he is not allowed to share in them. The essay of Wright's which he gives us to account for the genesis of *Native Son* has been overlooked in the interpretations of the conclusion, for in "How 'Bigger' Was Born" he writes that "the lawyer, Max, was placed in Bigger's cell at the end of the novel to register the moral—or what *I* feel was the moral—horror of Negro life in the United States" (*Native Son*, xxxiii). The moral horror of black life in America is that Bigger feels killing two helpless people is morally good. The truth is still unacceptable to many of the novel's critics.

Predictably, critic after critic has been swept away by the emotionality of the final scene and has misinterpreted Bigger's attitude toward the two murders. To distinguished scholar Houston A. Baker, Jr., Bigger "repudiates white American culture, affirms the black survival values of timely trickery and militant resistance, and serves as a model hero . . . for all readers of *Native Son* who possess the culture which provided maturation and value for Richard Wright."[10] By Baker's reasoning, every victim of social exclusion who turns into a homicidal maniac is heroic. Baker is so concerned with demonstrating the uniqueness of black folk culture and of showing its appearance in *Native Son* that he fails to pay attention to what the book actually says. About Bigger's relationship to black culture Wright is explicit: Bigger has rejected it; his jail scene with his mother is his only feeble nod to his existence as part of it. As far as white American culture is concerned, Bigger can hardly reject that which is not available to him. He is no Shine, Stackolee, or Dupree (black folk heroes) because he does not deceive anyone for very long but himself,[11] and because black folk heroes do not end up electrocuted by the white man.

A second representative critic is Lance Jeffers, who contends that "in prison he [Bigger] grows beyond moral blindness and crippled feelings."[12] In Jeffers's assertion he, like Baker, violates the text. Bigger's moral blindness may have been upgraded to the barely sighted "legally blind" category (in his acceptance that whites *can* be human; in his *tinge* of sadness at leaving a horrible memory of himself in his black community), but the change is hardly dramatic, for he would still need a cane to cross the street. What Jeffers cannot see or face at the book's conclusion is that though Bigger is *convinced* what he " 'killed for must've been good!' " (392), Bigger had to kill in order to ensure his own survival, although he is about to die.

It must be reiterated that the essential facts about Bigger's two killings are these: in the death of Mary Dalton, he was absolutely at the mercy of a conditioned response and in no way did he make a choice to kill: he held a pillow over her face to avoid detection by Mrs. Dalton; in doing so, he accidentally smothered Mary. In the premeditated murder of Bessie, Bigger acted only out of selfish motives: he was afraid she would give information about his first "crime" to the police. The burning of Mary and the terrifyingly gruesome killing of Bessie are profound indictments in this novel of social protest: America has given birth to a homicidal maniac. The killings by their very nature preclude the murderer's being morally admirable.

It does become part of Bigger's moral scheme, however, to consider himself in some sense heroic: "In all of his life these two murders were the most meaningful things that had ever happened to him. He was living, truly and deeply, no matter what others might think, looking at him with their blind eyes. Never had he had the chance to live out the consequences of his actions, never had his will been so free as in this night and day of fear and murder and flight" (225). Wright does not endorse his protagonist's self-judgment; he is presenting it as evidence in his protest against racial oppression: "In *Native Son* I tried to show that a man, bereft of culture and unanchored by property, can travel but one path if he reacts positively but unthinkingly to the prizes and goals of civilization and that one path is emotionally blind rebellion."[13]

Wright clearly indicates the distance between himself and Bigger: "He had been so conditioned in a cramped environment that hard words or kicks alone knocked him upright and made him capable of action—action that was futile because the world was too much for him. It was then that he closed his eyes and struck out blindly, hitting what or whom he could, not looking or caring what or who hit back" (225). Where Wright has no delusions about Bigger, his protagonist has many about himself. For instance, Bigger is convinced he will never be taken alive (250); but, when he is inevitably captured, he acts submissively, not heroically. How could it be otherwise, given overwhelmingly superior white power? Time after time, Wright establishes that Bigger is the victim of his own seductive imagination; and many readers have repeatedly accepted Bigger's own delusion that his actions must have been meaningful, good; but, more than anything else, they are simply *nothing*. Wright suggests America is producing nihilists in its Bigger Thomases. Hatred of the oppressor does not necessarily produce nobility: in *Native Son*, it produces a human being engaged in "emotionally blind rebellion,' " and, while such rebellion is surely emotionally and psychologically gratifying, its ultimate value is delusory, null and void.

It is possible, to an extent, to view Bigger as being at once a victim of environmental predetermination and a man resurrected by construing a dialectic that first regards the murders literally and then treats them symbolically. Seen as literal, actual events, both of his murders—the first, instinctive; the second, premeditated—are brutal, gruesome, horrible. But, if seen as metaphor, the killing of Mary Dalton represents the first time in Bigger's life that he has done something to the white culture that suffocates him, as he does Mary; and he has thus taken a step towards personal integrity. Though an accident, the first murder is transformed by Bigger into evidence of his manhood: he has at last acted, accomplished. The second killing, while not so significant to him as the first, is important for several reasons: it indicates his profound depravity, and it establishes that, if in a sense he killed by accident in the first instance, he is more than capable of violent, premeditated murder. Viewing this murder more symbolically, it does have a semblance of constructiveness, for, as has been previously noted, it represents Bigger's attempt to obliterate that meekness, that servility born of oppression, that he detects in himself no less than in Bessie; and the murder also fulfills a "deep psychological need to confirm the reality of the experience in Mary Dalton's bedroom."[14]

Both murders, viewed symbolically, do have "redeeming" aspects which, if and when they are realized by Bigger, could conceivably help him grow spiritually towards a fuller humanity. But regarding them as a moral and spiritual achievement is only possible if the murders are viewed *only* as a metaphor, which Wright surely did not intend. In both cases, Bigger kills women: Mary, when she is drunk; Bessie, when she is asleep. He will do anything to survive, however degraded. The superposition of symbolic heroism over his ugly deeds causes instinctive discomfort, and Morris Dickstein has discussed the problem of a symbolic interpretation of the novel in these illuminating terms: "*Native Son* moves from a crime-and-punishment plot to the story of how Bigger Thomas, by accepting his crime, achieves a measure of freedom and awareness—'what I killed for, I am.' But the theme and its material increasingly clash; the crime is finally *not* acceptable nor reducible to symbolism. Pursuing the matter, Wright's own liberated consciousness becomes too heavy, too subtle for Bigger, yet remains too entangled in the remnants of the murder plot to evade moral confusion."[15]

It is very difficult for some critics to admit that Bigger is a human monster, that he means nothing because the American culture that produced him itself means nothing. Bigger is a moral vacuum because America is; he is driven to his terrible deeds by a society that professes humane beliefs but actually operates on the basis of jungle ethics. Saunders Redding, a noted critic, explains why *Native Son* is rejected by so many readers, black and white: "They [blacks] did not want to believe that they were as helpless, as outraged, as despairing, as violent, and as hate-ridden as Wright depicted them. But they were. They did not want to believe that the America they loved had bred these pollutions of oppression into their blood and bone. But it had. 'Is this us? And is this our America?' It was."[16] Similarly, whites did not and do not want to acknowledge what their racism has produced.

But the matter is not so simple that the reader or the critic can say Bigger is a monstrous product of American racism and let it go at that. The real questions are these: is he an accurate literary recreation of what really exists in America's black ghettoes or is he a white fantasy? If the former is true, then is he all the truth or only part of a larger reality? The two portions of the first question are interrelated: Bigger is a fantasy and a reality simultaneously; it is because of the fantastical white stereotype that the reality exists. If people are treated as "niggers," as Bigger has been, some will indeed be brutalized, stunted beasts. On the other hand, as James Baldwin and Ralph Ellison have protested, Bigger is not representative of *all* black experience. Obviously the authors of *Native Son*, *Go Tell It on the Mountain*, and *Invisible Man* are not Bigger Thomases, but that does not mean they do not have a Bigger in their psyches, as Baldwin himself has acknowledged. The danger in taking the view toward Bigger that he is real is that the stereotype of the "nigger" may be confirmed by a white reader who may find evidence in the novel for his preconceptions. This particular book says, however, that, because of their treatment in America, black people have become, more or less, Bigger Thomases. Consequently, the racism that the book was meant to attack is confirmed or justified in a sense; but Wright clearly places the responsibility for this situation on whites.

III *Imagery and Symbol*

Throughout the narrative, Wright uses images and symbols to reinforce his discursive material. The important figures include the cross, whiteness, blindness, the ghetto and the city, the jungle, the beast. The cross symbol appears several times in different significations. To underline Bigger's rejection of his mother's otherworldly Christianity, Wright has Bigger tear off the crucifix around his neck at one point; and, at another, he throws it out of his prison cell. A second permutation on the meaning of the cross is generated when Bigger sees the fiery cross of the Ku Klux Klan burning on a building across from the Dalton home (the reader may wonder if the Dalton house would be located in a neighborhood where industrial buildings are across the road). The central emblem of Christianity has degenerated into an icon of hatred. The way Bigger is surrounded by policemen at his capture, with men holding his arms out, suggests a third implication of the cross: Bigger himself is being crucified by the society which produced him, but he is not in any other way a Christ figure.

Whiteness is used persistently as a representation of the fears and anxieties that are so much a part of Bigger's existence. The walls of the Daltons' kitchen are white; its tabletop is white, also. Not only is the dwelling white but so are its residents, including the ubiquitous cat, Kate. Mrs. Dalton's hair and dress are white;

Mr. Dalton also has white hair. Even the weather is symbolically suggestive: it begins to snow when Bigger runs from his employer's home at the discovery of Mary's remains in the furnace. When he realizes he will have to flee, "the insides of his stomach glowed white-hot" (207). He jumps out a window into a pile of snow: "Snow was in his mouth, eyes, ears; snow was seeping down his back" (207). The world is completely hostile to him; the Ogre itself, the white race, is, of course, of the same hateful colorlessness. Bigger is suffocating in a world of whiteness that denies his sense of self.

Closely related to whiteness is the blindness motif, one which is reiterated perhaps too often. Everyone in the novel is literally or figuratively sightless, from the state's attorney, Buckley, whose sight is obfuscated by virulent racism, to Mrs. Dalton, whose blindness is actual as well as iconic—in fact, Daltonism itself is a form of color blindness. No one in the book ever really *sees* Bigger; they see, instead, what they believe. They have been seduced by social stereotypes into seeing myth rather than the individual. To Bigger, all white people are alike because he is no more empirical in his judgment of whites than they are of blacks. Of the white characters, Jan *alone* begins to realize that the whites are blacks in white skins, that the blacks are whites in black skins. His insight helps in its turn to improve Bigger's vision, and he is eventually able to perceive Jan, at least, as a white individual.

Wright himself could never believe in racial mystique: "the secret of race is that there is no secret." Since racism and racial chauvinism have to be learned, they can also be unlearned. When blind people begin to see Bigger, he is worse than their most horrid prejudices indicated. But perhaps sensing that only by being visible to them does he have any chance of having the scales removed from his own eyes, Bigger finally desperately wants to lose his invisibility: "He wanted suddenly to stand up and shout, telling them [whites] that he had killed a rich white girl" (123). In his quest for visibility, he is like an animal driven by catastrophe from its woods into the human sphere—discovery leads inevitably to death. Bigger is, of course, blind to the truth of what will inevitably happen if he becomes visible, but he is no blinder than the culture of which he is a native son. Indeed, by using verbatim in his novel the venomous, blindly racist newspaper accounts of the case of an actual murderer named Robert Nixon, known as the brick slayer (*Quest*, 556, n. 4), Wright documents that point. When Wright is accused of sensationalism and exaggeration, his defenders can reply that, as a matter of fact, he often understates; for, compared to reality, *Native Son* is restrained.

The ghetto and the city are other dominant symbols. The black ghetto of Chicago is the jungle in which the black beasts live; and other beasts, the white ones, live in the surrounding areas. Chicago represents the urbanization of blacks and the consequent destruction of black folk values—such as intimacy with nature, appreciation of certain foods, and a strong sense of community—that had been nurtured in rural areas of the Bottom South. Chicago is Up South, the Promised Land that is exposed as a secular hell. Within this inferno, the ninth circle is the *South* side; and this area means poverty, violence, hopelessness, brutality. It is a prison where all the inmates are poor, black, deluded, frightened. Wright was the first black novelist to present with authority the urbanization of black experience. The environment is overwhelmingly the primary reality for Bigger: it is everything; he, nothing.

Wright employs unusually and extensively the presiding metaphor of Naturalistic fiction, the lawless jungle. When Buckley, the state's attorney in *Native Son*, summarizes the prosecution's case, he says, " 'Man stepped forward from the kingdom of the beast the moment he felt that he could think and feel in security, knowing that sacred law had taken the place of his gun and knife' " (373). In making this statement, Buckley unknowingly and ironically describes from the white point of view the world of Bigger Thomas and of America, for Bigger, a beast among beasts, is living in the wild forest. The discursive narrative line in the novel is developed, commented upon, and reinforced by Wright's use of images from man's primordial state, which, as Wright shows, still obtains in the white man's view of the black world.

The pattern of beast imagery informs the violent opening scene in which Bigger and his family awake to the sound of "a light tapping in the thinly plastered walls of the room" (8). A huge black rat finds itself trapped in the Thomases' one-room apartment: "The rat squeaked and turned and ran in a narrow circle.

looking for a place to hide; it leapt again past Bigger. . . . The rat's belly pulsed with fear. Bigger advanced a step and the rat emitted a long thin song of defiance, its black beady eyes glittering, its tiny forefeet pawing the air restlessly" (9-10). Bigger throws a skillet at the rat and then smashes its head with a shoe, which not only helps to establish the violent prospect of *Native Son* but also functions structurally in that this violence forestalls what Bigger will later do to Bessie and what will later happen to Bigger himself: he will be a black rat in the white man's world, and he will be running and looking desperately for a hole to crawl into (233). The rat is also used expressionistically to objectify Bigger's own fear and fury at finding himself trapped in a white world with no escape.

As in the oppressor's stereotype, the Thomas family "lives like pigs' " (15). Like a frightened animal, Bigger "lurked behind his curtain of indifference and looked at things, snapping and glaring at whatever had tried to make him come out into the open" (31). To Bigger's remark that he would like to go to the white nightclub in the movie *The Gay Woman*, Jack replies, " 'Man, if them folks saw you they'd run. . . . They'd think a gorilla broke loose from the zoo and put on a tuxedo' " (33). Buckley and the frenzied white mob refer to Bigger repeatedly as a "black ape." Wright has given his white readers one of their own projections—the black man as a murderous, depraved beast; but what most of the white characters in the book fail to realize, of course, is that they are more monstrous than Bigger because they share the ultimate responsibility for his being able to create and possess himself only through animal violence, only through cunning and fierceness.

The fearsome black rat in Bigger's own home finds its imagistic counterpart in the Dalton mansion in Kate, the ever-present white cat. When Mrs. Dalton walks down her hallway after briefly meeting her new chauffeur, "a big white cat, pacing without sound" (49), follows her; it looks at Bigger "with large placid eyes" (49). It is an intensified, animal image of the hostile white environment Bigger is in. Ironically, it is Mary, the liberal Communist sympathizer and daughter of the Daltons, who picks up Kate and carries her out of the room in which Mr. Dalton is questioning Bigger (54). The feline symbol of white guilt and hostility even watches Bigger while he tries to dispose of Mary's corpse:

> A noise made him whirl: two green burning pools—pools of accusation and guilt—stared at him from a white blur that sat perched upon the edge of the trunk. His mouth opened in a silent scream and his body became hotly paralyzed. It was the white cat and its round green eyes gazed past him at the white face hanging limply from the fiery furnace door. *God*! He closed his mouth and swallowed. Should he catch the cat and kill it and put it in the furnace, too? He made a move. The cat stood up; its white fur bristled; its back arched. He tried to grab it and it bounded past him with a long wail of fear and scampered up the steps and through the door and out of sight. Oh! He had left the kitchen door open. *That* was it. He closed the door and stood again before the furnace, thinking, cats can't talk. . . . (90)

Bigger can never escape Kate and all she represents: hostility, exclusion, fear. Bigger is Kate's prey; she will never give up the chase. While the newspaper reporters question Mr. Dalton about his missing daughter, Kate "leaped with one movement upon Bigger's shoulder and sat perched there. . . . He tried to lift the cat down; but its claws clutched his coat" (190). The white beast has caught Bigger and will devour him. Later, in Bigger's picture in the newspaper, Kate sits perched on his shoulder (210).

The contours of the second book, "Flight," are also largely determined by Wright's use of animal imagery. Mrs. Thomas remarks to her son, " 'You jumped like something bit you' " (96), when she sees him on the Sunday morning after Mary has been smothered, decapitated, and placed in the Daltons' furnace, which is like a fire-breathing dragon whose maw must be filled (174). Vera, Bigger's sister, sobs that her older brother makes her feel like a dog (99), while Buddy is described as being "like a chubby puppy" (103) that is no match for the monsters of the encircling white world. Bigger characterizes Bessie as a rabbit (137) who is always fearful and timid in the face of the possible consequences of fighting back against whites.

The black ghetto is the kingdom of the beast. Its streets are "long paths leading through a dense jungle, lit here and there with torches held high in invisible hands" (141). Staying in the old abandoned houses while hiding from the beast will be like " 'hiding in a jungle' " (214), Bigger says, for the old houses are rat-infested and dangerous. In the chase, Bigger corresponds to the fox or the hare; the white police, to the hounds. There is never any doubt that, like the rat in the opening scene, Bigger will be caught and killed, and he knows it: "This whole vague white world . . . was more than a match for him. . . . Soon it would track him down and have it out with him" (210). Finally about to be caught, he hides from the beast on top of a water tank, but a powerful jet of water forces him off: "The icy water clutched again at his body like a giant hand; the chill of it squeezed him like the circling coils of a monstrous boa constrictor" (251). To literalize the metaphor, the prey is being suffocated in the jungle. Later, at the inquest, Bigger wishes he had cheated the beast out of "this hunt, this eager sport" (291), by letting it kill him.

In "Fate," the last book of *Native Son*, Wright draws continually upon the source of his basic, informing metaphor, the kingdom of the beast. Bigger begins to accept it himself: "Maybe they were right when they said that a black skin was bad, the covering of an apelike animal" (256). The white newspapers exploit the simile relentlessly: " 'He looks exactly like an ape!' exclaimed a terrified young white girl. . . . His lower jaw protrudes obnoxiously, reminding one of a jungle beast. . . . All in all, he seems a beast utterly untouched by the softening influences of modern civilization. . . . He acted like an earlier missing link in the human species. He seemed out of place in a white man's civilization" (260). Max points out the metaphor to the judge: " 'It [the living corpse of black people] has made itself a home in the wild forest of our great cities, amid the rank and choking vegetation of slums! . . . In order to live it has sharpened its claws! . . . By night it creeps from its lair and steals toward the settlements of civilization! And at the sight of a kind face it does not lie down upon its back and kick up its heels playfully to be tickled and stroked. No; it leaps to kill!' " (362). When Buckley uses the same imagery in his summarizing speech, he does not or will not publicly admit that men like himself have made Bigger into a monster; he warns the court against other " 'half human black ape[s]' "; and he refers to Bigger as " 'a bestial monstrosity,' " a " 'black lizard . . . scuttling on his belly . . . over the earth and spitting forth his venom of death!' " (373). Later he calls Bigger a " 'black mad dog,' " a " 'rapacious beast,' " a " 'treacherous beast,' " a " 'coiled rattler,' " a " 'worthless ape,' " a " 'demented savage' " (374, 376-78). Of course, the height of irony is that Buckley calls Bigger names that are more applicable to the attorney himself, for he is a man who attacks and devours blacks in the South Side of Chicago, a man who preys on blacks to maintain his own political power.

Pervasive throughout *Native Son* is imagery from the kingdom of the beast, for Bigger is a "nigger," a black ape, a tiger stalking its white prey, as the stereotypical white racist notion has it. But in the wild, no other way exists but violence, the law of the jungle, for him to find himself and give himself some status. To survive in such a world, he must be a cunning and fierce animal, for his obeying the law will only exact his humanity as the price for submission—but his flouting the law will also leave him less than human. To be free, Bigger must, like a beast in the jungle, kill before he is killed, for in the kingdom of the beast, the only law is self-preservation. That kingdom is based on violence and is Wright's objective correlative for and his objectification of the whites' inner stereotypical vision of the black world. The prospect of *Native Son* is a jungle in which beast preys upon beast.

IV *General Assessment and Critical Reception*

Despite its flaws, *Native Son* is a remarkable book. The sheer power, the sheer compulsion of its narrative drive, is especially admirable, for no other American novel generates more narrative energy than does *Native Son*. In the first two sections, Wright's narrative is a juggernaut: nothing can stand in its way; the reader is practically forced to flow along. There is no time to withdraw in the first two sections because in two days Bigger has crushed a rat to death; planned a robbery; humiliated an acquaintance; taken an ominously disorienting job; killed, decapitated, and burned one woman; smashed in the head of another one with a brick; run frantically and finally been apprehended by 8,000 white men—the reader is always intensely engaged. Book three is inevitably anticlimactic because it is concerned with Bigger's trial rather than with an imaginative rendering of his life.

Since Wright knew intimately the South Side of Chicago as it existed in the 1920s and the 1930s, he is able to render impressively both the setting and the atmosphere. The squalor of the South Side was disgusting during the so-called good times, but it was still worse during the Depression. Her family on relief, Mrs. Thomas does menial work to pay the rent on their claustrophobic, one-room tenement. The season is winter, February and March, and Bigger is frequently cold and miserable, as well as hungry. Since he seems to have retained almost no remnants of the black folk culture of Mississippi in this barren Chicago ghetto—too poor in humanistic values to lend one of its youths even a scrap of humanity—Bigger is completely hopeless and closed to the possibility of human existence. Forced to live in a racially circumscribed area of the city, where rent and food prices are kept high, he is the perpetual outsider; nothing he can do will let him inside. Bigger exists as a nonintellectual version of Fyodor Dostoevsky's Underground Man in an atmosphere of dread, fear, and anxiety. The lovelessness that exists between him and his bleak, urban, antihuman world makes Bigger a nonman—what whites have always said blacks are.

In making a general assessment of *Native Son*, one finds oneself discussing the subject matter before discussing the technique. The subject matter of the book—the results of America's oppression of blacks—contains within itself much of the book's power.[17] Whereas in a writer like Henry James treatment is almost *all*, in *Native Son* the *donnée* is almost as important as the technique; and this point does not lessen Wright's achievement because he had the courage to choose the subject before any other writers did so. But his manner, not his matter, is the crucial consideration in the end. His literary technique is multiple: Socialist Realism, social protest, Naturalism, Gothicism, diatribe—he used any literary method he thought would work; he was no technical purist. And even though Realism and Naturalism, by the year *Native Son* was published, were beginning to be exhausted as literary strategies (indeed, they may seem quaint today if one thinks of Donald Barthelme, John Barth, and Thomas Pynchon—contemporary anti-Realistic novelists), given Wright's experience and consequent vision, such literary methods were his inevitable aesthetic, for, as he wrote in *Black Boy*, "all my life had shaped me for the realism, the naturalism, of the modern novel, and I could not read enough of them" (274). At its best, his Naturalistic-Realistic style renders in a visceral way the quality of Bigger's experience; for, with great immediacy, Wright makes one feel what it is like to freeze, to be extremely hot, to hate, to be uncontrollably afraid, to be terribly hungry. Wright's handling of the linguistic and nonlinguistic aspects of the first two books of *Native Son* is the pinnacle of his literary success.

Critical debate over *Native Son* is pronounced, and there is as yet no consensus over the novel as a whole, about its parts, or particularly its ending. The most provocative critical responses have come from James Baldwin, Ralph Ellison, Irving Howe, and Nathan A. Scott, Jr. In *Notes of a Native Son* in an essay entitled "Many Thousands Gone," Baldwin wrote that "the most powerful and celebrated statement we have yet had of what it means to be a Negro in America is unquestionably . . . *Native Son*. . . . We have yet to encounter . . . a report so indisputably authentic, or one that can begin to challenge this most significant novel."[18] But Baldwin then enumerates several objections to the book which, since the essay first appeared in *Partisan Review* in 1951, have been the basic design for a number of other patterns. For one thing, Baldwin believes that in Bigger Thomas Wright has given the reader a creature of his own imagination: Bigger is a myth rather than a social reality, or, if real, he has allowed white expectations about blacks to determine his identity. Hence, by killing Mary, Bigger created himself by acting according to white mythology. Baldwin also objects that, although "no American Negro exists who does not have his private Bigger Thomas living in the skull," Wright does not show how an equilibrium is maintained. Baldwin's case against *Native Son* in "Many Thousands Gone" is basically that Wright oversimplifies and that he tells only part of the truth. There is really no argument here, though, because Wright was purposely trying to tell only part of the truth in order to protest the injustice of it. Obviously, Wright and Baldwin are themselves examples of men who learned to contain their private Bigger Thomases or to unleash them creatively.

In another essay from *Notes of a Native Son*, originally published in 1949, "Everybody's Protest Novel," Baldwin wrote perceptively that Bigger's tragedy is that "he accepted a theology that denies him life, that he admits the possibility of his being subhuman and feels constrained, therefore, to battle for his humanity according to those brutal criteria bequeathed him at his birth."[19] Here Baldwin admits what many critics would not—that oppression can and does produce monsters, as Herman Melville suggested in *Benito Cereno*.

The debate between Irving Howe and Ralph Ellison also illuminates *Native Son*. In an essay entitled "Black Boys and Native Sons," Howe defended Wright from Baldwin's two essays on the grounds that Wright's Naturalistic protest, while narrow, made possible looser modes of fiction like Baldwin's *Go Tell It on the Mountain*. By releasing the full force of his rage, Wright made it impossible for the old lies that were based on minstrel and plantation traditions to be perpetuated; and, as a result, the publication of *Native Son* made a true black literature possible. Ellison took great exception to Howe: "Evidently Howe feels that unrelieved suffering is the only 'real' Negro experience, and that the true Negro writer must be ferocious."[20] Both critics are right: part of black experience in America is meaningless suffering, but that is not all black experience. It is the extension of *Native Son* to cover all black experience that is challengeable. The oppression of a minority will produce some monsters, but the monsters are not all the life of the minority, and they are also evidence of the monstrousness of the majority.

Nathan A. Scott, Jr., elaborated on Baldwin's view of *Native Son* in an essay entitled "The Dark and Haunted Tower of Richard Wright."[21] In his suggestively written piece, Scott contended that "the novel is controlled by precisely those hopeless assumptions about Negro life which elicited its rage, and its protagonist's sense of his own identity is formed by just that image of himself which, as it lives in the larger culture, has caused his despair." Neither Baldwin nor Scott can admit that what people think one is can be more important than what one actually is: what whites imagined Bigger to be, a monster, determined his act of "creation"—monstrous killings. Ultimately, the trouble with the famous criticisms of *Native Son* by Baldwin and Scott is that, since both write from a Christian viewpoint, neither believes that some experiences are meaningless: neither can accept that Bigger Thomas's life has not meant anything. Both reject Wright's desacralized view of human existence; in effect, they refuse to grant him his material and his vision.

CHAPTER 4

An Exile's Fiction

I *The Demon on the Cross*

THE Outsider (published in 1953) is an additional examination of two themes that Wright has been concerned with from the beginning of his career: misery and freedom. He begins the novel with two epigraphs to the work as a whole that immediately strike the note of suffering that is so persistent in his writing. The first quotation is from William Blake—"Cruelty has a Human Heart,/ And Jealousy a Human Face;/Terror the Human Form Divine,/ And Secrecy the Human Dress." This epigraph's unrelieved pessimism is underscored by the second one, which is from the *Book of Job*: "Mark me,/and be astonished, And lay your hands on your mouth." Wright has already used Job as the source of his inscription for *Native Son* and for *Black Boy*, and he employs it again for *Savage Holiday*, his next book.

For Book 1, Wright's epigraph is from Soren Kierkegaard; and he thereby signals his interest in Existentialism. The title of Book 1, "Dread," is an additional clue to the fact that Wright's several-year-old friendship with Jean-Paul Sartre and Simone de Beauvoir had led him to much philosophical speculation and that his proto-Existentialism in *Native Son* had at last developed and been scrutinized. "Dread" is the watchword of the German Existentialist Martin Heidegger, who believed it to be the Existentialist's *cogito*, the philosophical first step. Dread, the concerted consideration of reified Nothingness, is the only state in which a man can weigh the horror of the empty universe against the opportunity, in that void, to be exactly what he chooses. If there is Nothing, what is to stop him but his own faint heart? The result of Dread is Despair (which is the title of the penultimate book of *The Outsider*—it is a purgation of wishful thinking and a recognition that self-definition is the only definition possible in an empty universe).

But Wright's scrutiny of Existentialism did not leave him with an unalloyed approval of it. In *The Outsider*, the drawbacks rather than the advantages of freedom activate the author's imagination. The protagonist, Cross Damon (crucified demon) appears in the course of the novel to make the Existentialist leap to overcome almost all human restrictions—social, political, religious, moral; but he learns belatedly that, despite their arbitrariness, it is conventions that make one human. In dispensing with all regulation, Cross ironically becomes nothing and does not escape Nothingness. His life in the novel begins with sheer Existentialist Dread; but the despair with which he ends is of the garden variety rather than of the purifying, incandescent Existentialist species. Wright feels Cross's route of embracing Nothingness leads inevitably back to the Deep South where Black men, "outsiders," *are* nothing. He offers the reader in *The Outsider* his warning against too much freedom; for, if man can be anything he chooses, he is without form, a void. Since man needs shaping forces, he cannot accommodate complete freedom; and society cannot survive if it is comprised of men who declare themselves to be wholly liberated. Indeed, such completely free persons are equal in their menace to society to the completely enslaved Bigger Thomas of *Native Son*. The theme of Existential self-determination is an ambitious one, but it is unfortunately sullied through overuse by twentieth-century authors as well as by the melodramatic plot which attempts to advertise it.

As in "Big Boy Leaves Home," *Native Son*, and *Lawd Today*, the reader is first presented in *The Outsider* with a group of *bon vivants*; and, in this novel, all are post-office workers from the South Side of Chicago—one early indication among many that Wright was reworking and expanding the implications of his earlier *Lawd Today* as he wrote *The Outsider*. One of the postal clerks, Joe Thomas (an Uncle Tom), reports that somebody had said " 'that the best thing for Cross w-was to plow h-himself under.' "[1] This resonant and prospective irony preludes what Cross in fact accomplishes through his nihilistic blunderings as accurately as "Mr. Death" (2), the name given to Cross by another employee, intimates the path of carnage and suicide he will leave behind him.

When Cross throws money from the eleventh floor of the post office in order to watch people swarm antlike after it, he does so to signify his rejection of materialistic values—just as Fred Daniels in "The Man Who Lived Underground" rejects American society by stealing only the items he does not want. When speaking of two men who bumped heads diving after a quarter, Cross reveals another motivating force behind his action: he says (according to Joe) that that moment " 'was the only time he ever felt like God' " (5). And the narrator argues throughout the book that aspiration to divine power—to freedom from control by others—is basically what activates men, regardless of their ideology. On another occasion, Cross (the African Trickster figure who knows when to fool his adversaries may be vibrating in the background of the figure of Cross) plays a practical joke on his friend by forging magazine subscriptions; but Cross is also a forger on a grander scale—his life itself is a fraud. As Joe observes, " 'Any man who can do things like that is a man standing *outside* the world' " (6). Such "outsiderness," the book's presiding metaphor, is occasionally expanded so much that it becomes trivialized in meaning: " 'For four hundred years these white folks done made everybody on earth feel like they ain't human, like they're *outsiders*!' " (27).

By 1953, the year *The Outsider* was published, Wright had moved in his writing from the concrete to the theoretical, from the sociological to the philosophical. He now considered the condition of blacks in the Deep South to be the condition of all men everywhere: they were outsiders, outlaws, criminals who were standing outside the Chapel Perilous. Cross is a modern version of the quester who is seeking some source of value outside himself; but, in the waste land of the twentieth century, he finds none; and his personal life is a reflection of his metaphysical distress.

Wright interrupts the essentially linear action of the novel several times in the early sections of the book to present flashbacks that give the reader information about the three women who have helped to make Cross's life the disaster that it is—Dot, Gladys, and Cross's mother. The past impinges on the present throughout the book; for, although one of Cross's major objectives is to divorce himself from the past, and although Wright's faith in scientific determinism has been weakened to such an extent that he entertains the possibility of complete freedom, his novel as a whole exposes that concept as preposterous because of the formative power of history.

Cross's mistress, Dot, is pregnant by him but is young enough to bring a charge of rape against him if he refuses to marry her. His wife, Gladys, is a vindictive woman who is determined to exhaust his financial resources. He feels he is unable to confide his growing dread to either of these women or to his mother, who is severely disappointed with him. Dot, who has visited Cross's mother, has told her she is pregnant by her son; and she has also seen Gladys. As Cross prepares to visit his mother, the narrator observes that "this frigid world of the South Side in Chicago in February was suggestively like the one which his mother, without knowing it, had created for him to live in when he had been a child" (17); and such linking of scenery to states of mind is characteristic of Wright. Cross's childhood vision of God, bequeathed him by his mother, is of "an awful face shaped in the form of a huge and crushing NO" (18). " 'To think I named you Cross after the Cross of Jesus,' she [Cross's mother] moaned" (23). What she does not know is that her son is a scapegoat like Jesus, but not for the sins of mankind; for Cross is a martyr because he is an ethical outlaw who is betrayed by his own lust for power, the same lust he detests in others.

The pressure of the domestic situation builds until the only possible release is a violent one. Cross conceives of a plan whereby he will slap Gladys without apparent motivation in order to be rid of her. Ater twice experiencing this sadism, the terrified Gladys insists that he leave the house, which he does. But she also demands that he borrow $800 so she can clear the titles of the house and car. The environment is closing in on him, as it eventually does on nearly all of Wright's characters, but in this case its closing activates a tripspring of Existentialist freedom—rather than being beaten by environmental oppressions, Cross is forced by them into liberty.

Finch, the clerk with whom Cross transacts the loan, tells him, " 'You look like an accident going somewhere to happen' " (70). Wright's dramatic irony is seldom subtle, and this quotation is no exception, for Cross's subway accident is imminent. In a referential narrative that is struggling to be Surrealistic at this particular point, improbabilities and *dei ex machina* are perhaps not unexpected; but the subway accident strains Wright's Realistic-Naturalistic aesthetic. On the subway Cross "opened his eyes and noticed another Negro, shabbily dressed, about his own color and build, sitting across the aisle from him" (72). It is most convenient for Wright's purpose that Cross's double sit near him because he will be mistaken for the protagonist after the accident. Going underground in the subway recalls the early episode in *Black Boy* in which Wright hid under his parents' house, the kiln Big Boy hid in in "Big Boy Leaves Home," the Daltons' basement in *Native Son*, the sewer in "The Man Who Lived Underground," and the underground hallway of "The Man Who Went to Chicago." Wright's imagination found this metaphor irresistible.

Wright's representational narrative becomes momentarily nonobjective after the subway wreck that turns the coach upside down; for, when Cross flicks his lighter on, "Lines zigzagged and solids floated in shadows, vanishing into meaninglessness; images dissolved into other images and his mind was full of a sense of shifting significances" (74). The world is truly turned upside down; the metaphor has been literalized: his dead counterpart will be mistaken for Cross, so Cross can be reborn; his identity will now be what he chooses it to be rather than predetermined. In order to "free" himself from the wreckage of the subway and from his past, he must smash a *white* face with his gun: he will no longer allow whites to constrict him in their coils.

He considers himself fortunate to have survived; but, in reality, his descent into the hell of meaninglessness is beginning. His self-delusion is immense: "An intuitive sense of freedom flashed through his mind. Was there a slight chance here of his being able to start all over again? To live a new life? It would solve every problem he had if the world and all the people who knew him could think of him as dead" (83). The restaurant he enters after the accident is an old haunt, but the proprietor is absent, and the waitress is a new one, who "could not have known him from Adam" (83). Cross is hardly a new man and the world is certainly not Edenic after the subway crash, despite his Existentialist attitude that personal redemption is obtainable. The determinism of *Native Son* has given way to an examination of the concept that absolute freedom is a possibility, but Wright hardly supports total endorsement of it.

Cross's first new identity is Charles Webb; it is indeed a web of pretense that the protagonist weaves about himself throughout the narrative as he changes identities as casually as people change clothes. While the whole notion of identity has perhaps come to seem embarrassingly naive, Cross's continually exchanging one mask for another does suggest the fragile basis of the self. Because "He must sever all ties of memory and sentimentality, blot out, above all, the insidious tug of longing" (90), it seems highly unlikely that a man could become in a few days totally indifferent to the three sons he has loved and left at home. In order to "forge himself anew" (96) he decides to leave Chicago for New York; and "forge" is what he does, as he counterfeits everything about himself.

Cross's next role in his own play is John Clark. Like Rinehart in Ralph Ellison's *Invisible Man*, published the year before *The Outsider*, Cross conceives of selfhood as plastic, as a series of roles rather than as an essence. He watches his own funeral, really the one of his older self which he never really exorcises. Afterward, he begins to feel utterly alone and full of dread: "He was too much alone and it was unsupportable" (104). He has rejected the conventions, however arbitrary, that link men together in some type of communal warmth. When he accidentally encounters Joe Thomas, his friend from the post office, at a combination hotel-whorehouse, he kills him so that his escape from domestic responsibilities will not be blocked; and his first murder may suggest the destruction of his Jim-Crow antithesis. At the conclusion of the first book, Cross is described as being "free from everything but himself" (117).

Book 2, "Dream," centers around his "burden of nonidentity" (120). On the train taking him from Chicago to New York, he meets two people who will become important in his later experiences: Bob Hunter, who is trying to organize the porters for the Communist party, and Ely Houston, the District Attorney of New York City, who, because of the peculiar perspective on the world that his hunchback has given him, is also, like Cross, an outsider, and who recalls Boris Max in *Native Son* in that both are Wright's mouthpieces. Cross's deception persists as he tells Hunter that his name is Addison Jordan: "He had to be born again, come anew into the world. To live amidst others without an identity was intolerable" (132). Cross's final assumption of identity is Lionel Lane, a man who is dead, which suggests Cross's own spiritual collapse. This interpretation is supported by the fact that, when Hunter goes to see "Addison Jordan," the address Cross has given him is that of a funeral home.[2]

It is a cosmic or metaphysical identity that Cross is concerned with, not a racial, social, or national one. The conversation between him and Houston on the train is only the first of many, all of which give Wright the opportunity to indulge in speculation about what man is. During that first meeting, Cross tells Houston, " 'Maybe man is nothing in particular. . . . Maybe that's the terror of it. Man may just be anything at all' " (135). Wright's metaphysical generalities and platitudes are not always organically part of the text, but one of his biographers has shown that part of the blame for this weakness is the editors' because, by complying with their requests for cuts, Wright pared down the plot to melodrama while leaving the metaphysics exposed (*Quest*, 604, n. 35).

Cross, feeling guilty about giving Hunter a phony name, goes to see him in New York, and through Hunter he comes into contact with the Communist party, into which he is recruited by Gil Blount and Jack Hilton. Both are disagreeable characters: Gil "acts like a God who is about to create men. . . . He has no conception of the privacy of other people's lives" (174). And Gil easily comments, "We Communists do not admit any subjectivity in human life" (174). Since Wright does not make clear the reason that Cross would permit himself to be recruited for the party by such a man, Cross's decision seems insufficiently motivated; one suspects that Wright specifically wants to use such personalities not because they are convincing but because they are based on personalities that were abrasive to Wright when he was a Communist. In *The Outsider*, Wright is severely critical of the Communist party, which, though it had at one point helped him greatly, he had come to feel vindictive about because of its ruthless drive to power and its negation of individuality. After Hilton tells Bob Hunter that he is to stop organizing the Dining Car Waiters' Union, Gil tells the distraught Hunter, " 'Being a Communist is not easy. It means negating yourself, blotting out your personal life and listening only to the voice of the Party' " (183).

The Outsider's diatribes recall what Wright had already said in "I Tried to Be a Communist" and what Ralph Ellison had said about the Brotherhood (which has another Jack as one of its leaders) in *Invisible Man*.

In Book 3, "Descent," Cross goes to live with the Blounts in Greenwich Village, because Gil Blount wants to use him to desegregate his apartment building, which is managed by a Fascist, Langley Herndon. In this middle section, Cross becomes attracted to Eva ("Eve"), Gil's wife, a nonobjective painter who is married to a man who acknowledges only "objective" reality. In a creaking plot, one of the most mechanical incidents is Cross's discovery of Eva's diary; from it, he learns that Blount was ordered by the party to marry Eva because his doing so would add prestige to it. This discovery by Cross may reflect Wright's own dislike of being racially used by the Communists in Chicago to add luster to the party's image. Later on in the novel Wright embroiders on the party's perfidy that it extends to its own members—Gil's secretary, who is his mistress, is also spying upon him. Wright's rallying cry to his readers in all his books is that human beings must never be treated as less than respected members of the human race; he detests the abuse of party members by Communists as intensely as he hates white treatment of blacks in the deep South; and he equates the two.

Later, when Cross comes upon Gil and Herndon while they are fighting each other, he kills Herndon and then Gil, who, dying, falls toward a fireplace that recalls the Daltons' furnace: "flames danced and cast wild shadows over the walls" (226); "the winking shadows of the fire flicked warningly through the room" (227). And once again societal restriction fails to run apace of Cross's unharnessed, racing freedom; for Cross rearranges the room's evidence to make it indicate that the men have slain each other. Cross's demonism is most conspicuous in this sensational double murder, although in a mimetic narrative it may appear ludicrous. When Cross, who killed the two men partly out of disgust for their power mania, realizes that he has used their totalitarian methods in controlling them, Wright seems to be implying that man's drive for power is *the* motivating force in human nature.

In Book 4, "Despair," the environmental trap that had been sprung open by Cross's subway accident begins inexorably to close again. Though his previous existence was bedeviled by women, and though he eschewed all controls over his personal life when he fled Chicago, the reader is surprised to see Cross becoming more and more entangled with Eva, his strong feelings for whom are prominently advertised in this fourth section. In keeping with the morality play roles the women in *The Outsider* all seem to have, it is to Eva's house that Houston comes in order to investigate the deaths of Gil and Herndon; and as Houston's investigations assume more and more importance in the story, the reader, after also having read *Native Son*, realizes how much Wright's fiction owes to the conventions of the detective story.

Cross, unmindful of Houston's activities, becomes furious at Hilton because he is having Bob Hunter, an illegal alien, deported to a Trinidad prison. He goes to argue with Hilton and, in one more of a series of incredible coincidences, arrives at Hilton's hotel room when he is absent; and a maid, who is cleaning the room, permits Cross to enter. There he finds his own lost handkerchief, smeared with his latest victims' blood, and realizes that Hilton has casually carried Cross's fate in his hands for some time. When Cross recognizes in Hilton a fallen angel like himself, he knows that "the only difference between him[self] and Hilton was that his [Cross's] demonism was not buttressed by ideas, a goal" (291). Cross is driven only by an inchoate desire to authenticate himself; Hilton has the narrower, more available goal of Communist domination. While Cross waits for Hilton to return to his hotel room, he listens to jazz, which Wright considered suggestive of wild, uncontrollable feeling amidst a highly regulated society. When Hilton arrives he tells Cross that " 'what you see before your eyes is all there is' " (299). The acceptance of such radical reductionism, leading surely to the perception of all values as arbitrary, results in the kind of demonism that Wright detects in Nihilism and in Communism. Tradition and custom, however capricious, do preclude the formation of Cross Damons and Hiltons. In an earlier, racial protest period, Wright's efforts were focused on an attack on tradition and custom, but he now defends them. According to Tony Tanner's thesis in *City of Words*, this vacillation would place Wright squarely in the tradition of much American fiction since World War II which, Tanner contends, is obsessed with the problem of too much versus too little freedom.

At any rate, Cross shoots and kills Hilton, taking care to make the murder appear to be a suicide. Houston's description of Cross after his fourth murder summarizes what Wright feels that an outsider represents: " 'Could there be a man in whose mind and consciousness all the hopes and inhibitions of the last two thousand years have died? A man whose consciousness has not been conditioned by our culture? A man speaking our language, dressing and behaving as we do, and yet living on a completely different plane? A man who would be the return of ancient man, pre-Christian man? Do you know what I mean?' " (316).

Although Cross tells Eva he killed Hilton and although he confesses his other murders to her, she thinks he is delirious and refuses to believe him; and he almost kills her to protect her from his own monstrousness. In his attempt to destroy totalitarianism, he has become tyrannical himself; and he represents Wright's own fear of what was happening in the West in the 1950s during the years when many Americans searched unrestrainedly for Communists. Three men come to Hunter's apartment, where Cross is now staying, to question him: Menti, Hilton's assistant; Hank, a thug; and Blimin, the party's Grand Inquisitor. For fifteen pages (353-67) Wright speaks *in propria persona*, although the speaker's name is Cross; and this entire section would fit snugly in Wright's *White Man, Listen*! or in *The Color Curtain*. This long disquisition indicates that man tries to give a human meaning to what is utterly indifferent to him; but, since science and industrialization are destroying human values, men are becoming, like Cross Damon, outsiders.

Early in Book 5, "Decision," the final section, appears a statement which summarizes Cross's predicament: "He knew that he had cynically scorned, wantonly violated every commitment men owe, in terms of common honesty and sacred honor, to those with whom they live. That, in essence, was his crime" (374). In a sense, then, Cross is an elaboration of Bigger Thomas, another urban demon whose life meant only nothing. In the meantime, Houston has managed to refit the pieces of the life that was fragmented when its sustaining identity was obliterated: he knows his real name, his former employment, even of the subway accident; and he confronts Cross not only with these, but also with the specter of his dead mother (killed by hearing of her son's deeds). Cross has now killed four men, caused the grieving death of his mother, and is about to cause the suicide of Eva. All this is excessive, but it does demonstrate how far he has moved beyond conventional behavior—so far, in fact, that he shows almost no sign of emotion when Gladys and his three sons appear in Houston's office.

After Eva learns about him from Menti and Blimin, Cross acknowledges that he killed Gil, Herndon, and Hilton. Because his deceptions are too much for Eva to assimilate after having been deceived into marrying Gil, she leaps from the Hunters' apartment window. At this point in the narrative, the reader discovers what Cross had been reading before he began living his nihilism: Friedrich Nietzsche (the epigraph to Book 5 is also to Nietzsche), G. W. F. Hegel, Karl Jaspers, Martin Heidegger, Edmund Husserl, Soren Kierkegaard, and Fyodor Dostoevsky (421). These thinkers—variously Existentialist, nihilistic, and atheistic in their espousals—brought Cross to the edge of reality: he is no longer human in the sense that humanness is based on ritual, convention, custom, tradition. Houston knows such a person killed Gil, Herndon, and Hilton, but he cannot prove it. Consequently, he "frees" his suspect, but Cross is shot either by Menti, Hank, or both of them. Dying, Cross is asked by Houston what he found in life: " 'Nothing. . . . Alone a man is nothing' " (439). Though Existentialist thought has offered Cross an intellectual rationale for his attitudes, the action of the novel shows the ultimate rejection of that philosophy, at least as it is presented in *The Outsider*. Cross's final speech implies that Wright had come to believe in the necessity of the social conventions even if they have no absolute sanction.

The Outsider represents a distinct shift away from *Lawd Today*, *Native Son*, and *Black Boy* in its racial emphasis. Unlike the earlier works and anticipating the subsequent *Savage Holiday*, in which all the characters are white, both the narrator and the protagonist of *The Outsider* disavow any interest in race: "There was no racial tone to his [Cross's] reactions; he was just a man, *any* man who had had an opportunity to flee and had seized upon it" (86). And Cross, musing about Eva, wonders, "Could he [Cross] allow her to love him for his color when being a Negro was the least important thing in his life?" (288). While these assertions may be true, it has been suggested that *The Outsider* is still a novel of race;[3] and there are unquestionably a number of instances in which race is of specific importance. When, for example, Cross wants a birth certificate for one of his new identities, Lionel Lane, he assumes the guise of a humble, shuffling "darkie." Eva Blount's attraction to him is originally based on the assumption that, because he is black, he is deceived. Gil Blount, Eva's husband, sees him as an opportunity to challenge residential segregation. And there is tokenism in the Communist party's desire to include him in its structure. Moreover, the whole notion of freedom obviously has a more immediate significance for blacks than for many whites: "That all men were free was the fondest conviction of his life" (87). Unfortunately, the quality and the amount of his freedom, except that it is not exclusively racial, is never convincingly mediated by the novel.

Other comparisons between *The Outsider* and Wright's earlier works are more cut and dried, however, than is the degree of racial consciousness from one to another. For instance, one is certainly struck by and disappointed with the flaccid prose of *The Outsider* when it is compared with the much more powerful language of *Black Boy* and *Native Son*. Where *The Outsider* is abstract in diction, the other two are concrete, specific, vivid. The resonance and imaginative power of these two works are impressive, but *The Outsider* is thin in texture, lacks suggestiveness, is too explicit, too obvious, too discursive, and too expository. The crisp, direct syntax of *Black Boy* has given way to loosely organized sentences and paragraphs in *The Outsider*, and even more disappointing in that later work are such painfully embarrassing passages of prose as the following: "Slowly, so slowly that no one could notice anything, he moved his bare elbow to and fro across the tip of her breast, realizing with sensual astonishment: She's not wearing a brassiere!" (30). Wright, who can do much better, is usually above "sleazy cheesecake"; but the fact that he indulges in it reveals that he can let his writing go on automatic pilot.

Even if one takes into consideration the problems Wright had with the editing of *The Outsider*, it remains a major disappointment, for it is such an ambitious novel that its flaws are very conspicuous—melodramatic plot, thin characterization, bad writing, sermonizing and haranguing by the author. Wright had become in the 1950s too much the philosopher to remain faithful to experience itself. Much of *The Outsider* reads like a primer of the clichés of Existentialism rather than a powerful dramatization of the *events* and *people* behind the philosophizing. Wright was always at his best when he allowed events to reveal meaning instead of trying to impose meaning on events, as he did in *The Outsider*.

II *Freud and Savage Holiday*

The third novel Wright published, *Savage Holiday* (1954), is without question his most disappointing one. Although the tendency in contemporary criticism is to find merit in practically everything, *Savage Holiday* is beyond any doubt the fiction that belongs in a sleazy drugstore book-stack. While it was rejected by Wright's usual publisher, Harper, and while it was never published in hardcovers but was a paperback original, this book is notable as Wright's single novel that is not primarily concerned with black characters; race is mentioned in the narrative, but all the major characters are white.

Dedicated to Clinton Brewer, a man who killed two women because of his psychological difficulties (*Quest*, 237), *Savage Holiday* is concerned with the murder of Mrs. Blake by the protagonist, Erskine Fowler, to whom she strongly recalls his mother. As a result of this and other incidents, the too-obvious Freudian implications seriously damage the book. The epigraphs to the entire novel are taken from Job and from Oscar Wilde's *The Ballad of Reading Gaol*—they again underscore the theme of human suffering; but the use of Wilde suggests the common boundary that sexuality and human misery all too often share. The three inscriptions to Part I, "Anxiety," (from *Exodus*, *Sunday Neuroses* by Sandor Ferenczi, and *Totem and Taboo* by Sigmund Freud) explain the title: Sunday, an intended day of piety, can be a holiday on which dark, primordial forces from the id are released. The use of alliterative words for titles of the sections of his novels has by now become a habit of Wright's; and, true to form, the titles in *Savage Holiday* are "Anxiety," "Ambush," and "Attack."

The narrative begins with one of Wright's notoriously heavy-handed ironies: forty-three-year-old Erskine Fowler, a thirty-year employee of the Longevity Life Insurance Company, is now being fired to make room for the president's son—but the red, white, and blue banner at his "retirement" banquet announces that Longevity Life "brings security to you and your survivors."[4] More dramatic irony appears when the president of the company, describing himself as "head of this family" (13), commends Fowler as " 'a Mason, a Rotarian, a Sunday School Superintendent' " (12)—for his severance has left Fowler a dangling man, an outsider who is dangerously filled with dread.

Before Fowler responds to the president's words, he runs "his left hand tensely inside his coat (as though touching something)" (13); and the reader discovers later that this gesture, repeated frequently, is to touch a set of four automatic pencils that Fowler seems to have with him always. This compulsive action, which is eventually explained in terms of his Oedipus complex, serves the narrative function of creating suspense. Fowler's opening remarks—" 'My command of words is meager. Action is my forte' " (16)—foreshadows that, by the end of the novel, he accidentally will have caused the death of little Tony Blake and will have murdered his mother Mrs. Blake by repeated stabs in the stomach with a butcher knife.

Appropriately, Fowler has been selling insurance (as Wright himself had) because "insurance was life itself; insurance was instinctively and intuitively knowing that man was essentially a venal, deluded, and greedy animal" (28). Unfortunately and ironically, he does not apply this wariness about insurance to himself; he knows man is a guilty creature, but his own ambivalent feelings of guilt toward his mother are so repressed that they can be dealt with only by an act of savage exorcism. Although Wright has maintained suspense by revealing gradually the full extent of the protagonist's Oedipus complex, the importance of that psychological problem lies in Wright's earlier emphasis on the presentness of the past; for, just as 300 years of slavery resulted in Bigger Thomas, Fowler's earlier relationship with his mother impels him to befriend Tony and to kill Mrs. Blake. Wright's explanation of present problems is always environmentalist, but *Savage Holiday* is also informed by another of Wright's favorite themes, too: freedom. Like Cross Damon, Fowler feels existentially free: "He was trapped in freedom" (33). The paradox leads to Fowler's disintegration, for, without his job, his routine, his customs and habits, he becomes a savage beast who is at the mercy of an Oedipus complex.

One example of the many coincidences the reader almost expects in Wright is that in this novel an exact duplicate of Fowler's relationship with his mother appears in Fowler's neighbors in his Manhattan apartment: Mrs. Blake, a prostitute, lives alone with her son Tony, for the father and husband had died in World War II. Fowler lost his own father when he was a little boy, and his mother was a prostitute. Wright's fondness for the device of dreams, seen in *Lawd Today* and in *Native Son*, is used here to advertise, in a too-consciously Freudian direction, perhaps, Fowler's subconscious fear of sex either with his mother or with Mrs. Blake. He dreams he is in a deep forest when he hears the sound of an ax: "he peered cautiously and saw a tall man swinging a huge ax chopping furiously into a v-shaped hollow of a giant tree and the chips were flying and the man's face was hard and brutish and criminal-looking" (37). Fowler would have liked to sleep with Mrs. Blake, but, because many other men have, he hates her. His refusal to acknowledge his repressed sexuality is belied by his appearance when he is naked: "He stripped off his pajamas and loomed naked, his chest covered with a matting of black hair, his genitals all but obscured by a dark forest, his legs rendered spiderlike by their hirsute covering. Tufts of black hair protruded even from under his arms. Nude, Fowler looked anything but pious and Christian" (40-41).

In order to get his Sunday paper, Fowler enters the hall without covering his hairy nakedness, and his apartment door slams shut and locks. Constance Webb reports that this incident is based on an event that piqued Wright's imagination, for he had "read a short piece in the Paris edition of the *Herald-Tribune*. A New York businessman had been trapped nude in the corridor of his elegant apartment building. In the man's predicament Richard saw hints of terror and fear similar to the daily state of mind of the black man."[5] Wright transformed the incident into an emblem of Fowler's total exposure: his eminent respectability has been replaced with panic at his state of primitive reversion. The episode dramatizes modern man's overwhelming anxiety when social conventions have collapsed; he goes on a savage holiday. The veneer of civilization is thin.

Fowler's atavistic, sexual appearance is not only a metaphor but a *deus ex machina* in the plot. In order to reenter his apartment, Fowler goes to Mrs. Blake's balcony, which is just below his open bathroom window. The sudden appearance of a naked man frightens Tony, who is playing on the balcony, and causes him to fall off his electric hobby horse onto the balcony rail and then ten floors to his death. Tony's panicked response recapitulates Fowler's when he was a child: he often saw naked men "fighting" with his mother and consequently feared them. Wright suggests his meaning in a passage that reduces his narrative to textbook Freud: "These days everybody was talking about 'complexes' and the 'unconscious': and a man called Freud (which always reminded him of *fraud*!) was making people believe that the most fantastic things could happen to people's feeling. Why, they'd say that he'd gone *deliberately* onto that balcony like that, nude" (61).

Mrs. Blake suspects Fowler is responsible for her son's death, but Fowler is not certain that she knows he is the cause. She does claim she saw a pair of naked feet dangling over the balcony below Fowler's bathroom window. An element of detective fiction is apparent here as Wright relies on Fowler's anxiety over whether Mrs. Blake knows, to propel the reader through the narrative.

Part 2, "Ambush," opens with Fowler's wondering, anguished, how he is to contend psychologically with the child's death: though the concealment of his part in Tony's plunge is inimical to him, he knows that even if he confesses to scaring Tony, he will feel guilty—and feeling guilt or, indeed, *any* emotion, fills him with panic. "From puberty onwards he had firmly clamped his emotions under the steel lid of work and had fastened and tightened that lid with the inviolate bolts of religious devotion. Now he felt ambushed, anchored in a sea of anxiety, because he was tremblingly conscious of all his buried demons stirring and striving for the light of day" (80).

He draws back from this glimpse into his maimed psyche by retreating to religion—"He was convinced that in the end his faith in God would lead him to a solution" (82), and, gratifyingly, at the Mount Ararat Baptist Church, he believes that he is "given the Word" that Tony's fall was a part of God's plan to force Mrs. Blake to confess her sins. However, even at the moment he believes he hears God's voice instructing him about his sister in

Christ, Fowler's imagination is creeping into distinctly unbrotherly realms: "his consciousness was seduced by the persistent image of Mrs. Blake's nude, voluptuously sinful body which he had glimpsed twice through his open window" (89-90).

There are clearly no religious forces that can sever Fowler's bondage to his tumultuous, confused Oedipal feelings about Mrs. Blake: "He yearn[s] to believe that she [is] as innocent as a boy believes his mother to be" (138)—he hungers to marry her—he itches to harm her. Nor, in this Wrightian version of Freud, can the protagonist hope to rely on the rationality that he possesses in good measure to calm his roiling ego and id. He knows that "this woman was objectifying some fantasy in his own mind, just as he had objectified a fantasy in the mind of poor little Tony" (178); yet despite his understanding, he is as fatally subjected to the fantasy as was the unfortunate youngster.

In musing about the child's panicked response to adult male nudity, Fowler travels by way of flashback to another episode in Tony's life which suggests all too plainly that, had the boy lived to maturity, he would have been as psychologically crippled as his neighbor. He recalls that Tony had once told him that his mother "fought" with naked men, and that the result was a baby. Consequently, when Fowler bought Tony two toy bombers, the boy pretended that the fighting between them produced baby bombers. More important than merely highlighting the disturbances in the mind of an already-dead youngster, this anecdote once again advertises the substitution of violence for love in American society, one of the most persistent themes in all of Wright's work and prominent from "Big Boy Leaves Home" through some of the stories in *Eight Men*. And significantly, what little sex appears in this novel of repressed sexual desire is tawdry: "As she [Mrs. Blake] continued to weep, a part of her left breast showed and he could see a dark reddish tint encircling the nipple, glowing like a shy shadow through her nylon brassiere" (120).

In Part 3, "Attack," Fowler's "demons" exhume themselves for a *Walpurgisnacht* revelry when Mrs. Blake first unbalances Fowler by telling him that he reminds her so much of Tony—that he needs a mother; and then sends him reeling by admitting that she did not love Tony and that she is not maternal by nature. In quick response, Fowler confesses the whole tragedy in a scene rife with emotional reverses from love to hatred, and stabs her to death. At the police station, he realizes the signficance of his compulsion to touch the four automatic pencils when emotional pressure increases: as a child he had imagined that his mother would say that he was bad if the picture he had drawn with colored pencils of a "dead," battered doll was reported to her. He feared the accusation that he had murdered the doll; and he hated his mother.

Savage Holiday shows that Wright tended to arrive late. As noted earlier, Wright, in the 1930s, was influenced by Naturalism, long after Frank Norris, Stephen Crane, and Theodore Dreiser's heyday; in the 1950s, he was writing a Freudian narrative, but Freud's influence had been at its height in literature in the 1920s. The time lag in both cases was about thirty years.

III *Return of the Native Son*

The first novel in a planned trilogy, *The Long Dream* (1958) is the only volume to have been published; but five episodes from the second, "Island of Hallucinations," have also appeared. *The Long Dream* is set in the Deep South; but, if the reader assumes that the book signals Wright's return to his roots, the assumption is valid only if this first volume of the trilogy is regarded apart from "Island of Hallucinations," which is set in France. The central concern of *The Long Dream*, his fifth novel, is the relationship between a black man, Tyree Tucker, and his son, Fishbelly (called Fish), who live in a town of 10,000 blacks and 15,000 whites. Since Wright's town in the novel is Clintonville, Mississippi, and since he sets the time as the late 1930s and the 1940s, the reader senses that Wright's memories of Jackson vibrate underneath the surface of *The Long Dream*.

The title suggests that for three and a half centuries blacks in America have deluded themselves by thinking that they could eventually live as human beings; and the implication of the novel is that this dream will remain a nightmare. Although flight may be the only solution, a black may remain nothing even *after* flight. The central metaphor of the book is the analogy between black existence in America and illusion, dream, delusion.

Part One, "Daydreams and Nightdreams," which depicts Fish's

childhood, contains the first step of his initiation into reality in this *bildungsroman*. One of Fish's major concerns is the white woman, Cleaver's Ultrafeminine; for, even as a child, Fish's existence is violated by this sexual enthrallment: "He went down the hallway and into the office and sank into his big armchair, feeling his tiny legs dangling to the floor. He had blundered into the mysterious world that grownups hid from children and now he was praying that that world would be forgiving, merciful. . . . On the wall was a calendar that held a photo of a laughing white girl strolling along a sandy beach, her blond hair blown back, her lips holding a cigarette, her legs as white as bread, and her rounded breasts billowing under satin. . . ."[6] The same temptation appears frequently throughout the book; and Fish's mistress, Gladys, is light enough to "pass." He literally internalizes his ambivalent feelings about the white woman by eating a newspaper picture of one after the police have arrested him, for he fears the consequence of their finding the picture in his possession. If white women are symbols of freedom, then Fish would be inevitably attracted to them since America is a prison to him.

One of Wright's old mannerisms—telling the reader what he has already shown him—betrays the novelist repeatedly in the first part. When one of Fish's boyhood friends, Tony, tells Fish and two other pals, Zeke and Sam, that blacks are just like everybody else in America, the author intrudes to tell the reader that "Tony tried to make black life in America seem normal" (34). Since the dialogue has already made this observation evident, Wright's comment is a redundancy. In fact, he is so anxious for the reader to understand his point that his reader frequently has the feeling that an episode is planted in the narrative to make a racial point rather than as an organic incident. Polemics frequently precede art in *The Long Dream*.

The theme of racial self-hatred is strongly emphasized in the first part of the novel. Fishbelly spits at his own reflection; and, when he and his pals later attend a farm fair on "Colored Folks' Day," they throw baseballs at a "nigger" head. Fish's response is characteristic: "That obscene black face was his own face and, to quell the war in his heart, he had either to reject it in hate or accept it in love. It was easier to hate that degraded black face than to love it" (46). The name Fishbelly, suggesting as it does disagreeable, dead, chalky whiteness, is Wright's ironic comment upon, and response to, these feelings. Inevitably, a white woman intrudes at the fair, this time in the person of a show girl who, while "unbuttoning her blouse and baring her big white breasts in the half-light" (47), tells the boys she will take them into her trailer for five dollars apiece. Such lurid depiction of sex is, as before, an embarrassment even to Wright's admirers.

Probably the most shocking event that Fish experiences during his transition from childhood to adulthood is the killing of Chris (Christ?) Sims, a black youth who is slain by Clintonville's whites for being in the same room with a white woman. When Fish watches the corpse as his father, who is an illiterate mortician in the black community, and another character named Dr. Bruce examine it, "Fishbelly saw a dark, coagulated blot in a gaping hole between the thighs and, with a defensive reflex, he lowered his hands nervously to his groin" (77).

The theme of manhood—physical, racial, moral, economic—is, of course, a central one in Wright's literature from *Uncle Tom's Children* (1938) to *Eight Men* (1961). In denying manhood to Chris by slicing off his genitalia, the whites terrify the young Fish; and he later faints when the white police threaten to castrate him. But Wright implies in *The Long Dream* and elsewhere that the worst emasculation of the blacks by the whites takes place above the eyes rather than below the belt; for Fishbelly is all too ready to accept white culture's definition of him as a nonman, a "nigger." He and his companions compensate for their own sense of inferiority by treating Aggie West, an effeminate black youth, the same way whites treat them—as subhuman. In Wright's view, a position that may date the novel, published in 1958, survival and manhood are not simultaneous possibilities for blacks in America.

The initial section of *The Long Dream* concludes with an incident that forces Fishbelly from innocence into the actual world in which his father, Tyree, tries to survive. In a pastoral setting that recalls one of the opening scenes of "Big Boy Leaves Home," Fish's gang agrees to a mudball fight with a rival gang: "They [Fish and his pals] lolled upon the grass, their eyes sheltered against the sun dazzle. A bumblebee droned past. A grasshopper jumped, vanished behind a leaf. Sam plucked a weed stalk from the ground and began nibbling thoughtfully at it" (104). The boys are in harmony with nature, but white intruders, this time two policemen, always come to destroy the idyllic atmosphere. And yet Fish is "fatally in love with that white world, in love in a way that could never be cured" (158).

A gruesome nightclub fire in the middle part of the novel, "Days and Nights," reiterates the paradox that what often seems in Wright most sensational or exaggerated is in fact a restrained version of a fantastical reality. The fire at the Grove, as it is called in the novel, which kills forty-two people, including Fish's girlfriend Gladys, is based on the actual burning of the Rhythm Nightclub in Natchez, Mississippi: but the novelistic fire is "planted" by the author in order to allow him to dramatize the relationship between Tyree, Cantley, and Dr. Bruce. Cantley, the chief of police, is a business partner of Tyree in such illegitimate ventures as a whorehouse and graft; Dr. Bruce, the owner of the Grove, retains Tyree as, euphemistically, a "silent partner": Tyree is, in fact, a henchman for Dr. Bruce, who is paid to pass on "hush money," implausibly in the form of personal checks of Tyree's, from Bruce to Cantley in order to keep Cantley quiet about Bruce's club's violations of the fire code.

In a referential, representational narrative, the checks do not seem credible because the conspirators would have used cash to avoid written records and to preserve anonymity; but, according to his custom, Wright sacrifices faithfulness to facts in order to instruct the reader. The canceled checks assume the status of Edgar Allan Poe's purloined letter, for melodrama and detective work become the major centers of interest at this place in the narrative. Tyree has long suspected that the checks will some day come in handy for him and he has left them secretly in the safekeeping of Gloria, his mistress. When Tyree faces indictment for the fire at the Grove, he realizes he can no longer avoid making the existence of the checks known. He decides to put the checks, and his fate, into the hands of a white reformer, McWilliams. The unrealistic loftiness of McWilliams's standards is adumbrated by his diction—he uses words like "foul" and "dastardly" (282) in a stiff and unnatural manner. His idealistic misunderstanding of the pervasiveness of the corruption in Clintonville causes him to send the incriminating checks to the grand-jury foreman the evening before the grand-jury inquest, as formal rules dictate; but his "correct" action is a world away from what common sense might have told him to do. The checks are predictably intercepted on their trip to the foreman, leaving Tyree with no ammunition to use against Cantley and, consequently, at his mercy. Tyree's misunderstanding is as deep as McWilliams's—his greatest fear now is that Cantley, possessing the checks, will also want Tyree's money: Tyree vows he will kill before he will lose it. But Cantley wants nothing as minor as Tyree's money—he wants his life. When Tyree is mortally wounded in an ambush arranged by Cantley, he exults as he dies that his money is safe.

By now, Fish is unable to avoid facing the fact that his father used the same racist system that oppressed him to oppress his fellow blacks; for Wright never ceased indicating the oppression of the oppressed by their own. Fish himself, though willing to exploit and damage his culture, responds emotionally to it in a way that is a recapitulation of Wright's response in *Black Boy*. Fish "sensed in them [blacks] a profound lassitude, a sort of lackadaisical aimlessness, a terribly pathetic range of emotional activity veering from sex to religion, from religion to alcohol" (199). Wright implies that the black community is in a long dream and that it is refusing to face the ultimate futility of all responses to white racism. Everything Tyree, Fish, Gloria, and the other black characters do finally leads to frustration because they can do nothing that will even threaten the system of racism.

All this while, Fish, who has been Tyree's understudy, has been preparing to manage his father's business—to be a funeral director, a rent and graft collector, a whorehouse investor. In the novel's final section, "Waking Dreams," Fish realizes how fully he has now inherited the enterprises when he awakens to find no difference between his nightmares and the pedestrian world. Cantley's fears now focus on him because he correctly assumes there may be more canceled checks and that Fish may have them. Fish does in fact get them during a joint funeral for his murdered father and the nightclub fire victims; his receipt of the canceled checks from Gloria formally signals his succession to his father's troubles. Gloria, who is never discovered as the one-time keeper of the checks, flees north to Memphis with Dr. Bruce, leaving Fish the sole object of Cantley's wrath. Cantley has him framed and jailed on a charge of raping a white woman—an irony, because Fish has frequently imagined such a rape; and Cantley leaves Fish in jail for two and a half years. Again ironically, the system of intimidation that Cantley has used for power and profit precludes his discovering the truth about Fish's ownership of the checks; for Fish, who is uncertain as to whether or not Cantley will kill him if he admits to the possession of the checks, doggedly denies knowledge of them and continues to languish in jail. Being in jail is, however, not so much of a hardship and not so much of a change in Fish's situation: he has been in a metaphorical prison all his life.

Finally, when Cantley stops his search for the checks and Fish is let out of jail, he flees north to Memphis, to New York City (where he stays only briefly), and then to Europe to join his old pals, Zeke and Tony, who are in the American army stationed in France. On the flight to Paris, Fish sits next to an American who is flying to Italy to see his father's hometown: "That man's father had come to America and had found a dream: he had been born in America and found a nightmare" (380). Fishbelly is another "native son" who is rejected by the same world that made him: he is a fish out of water. From Europe, when he sends a letter containing the checks to McWilliams, he concludes that "all of his bridges to the past would be destroyed" (382). Given Wright's emphasis on the presentness of the racial past, Fish is still deluded, gulled, a fish.

Like Bigger, Fishbelly has fled the Bottom South; but he arrives in Paris rather than in the traditional black "haven," the American ghetto. Relative to other provocative differences between *The Long Dream* and *Native Son*, Bigger Thomas is fatherless and is only in a casual sense a part of the black community; and Fishbelly, precisely because he has a father who is a respected member of the black community, is much more a part of his culture, but riddled with negative feelings about it. And, while *Native Son* is a powerfully suggestive narrative, *The Long Dream* is thin and episodic, suffering from a plethora of incident. Both novels are about violence, but the violence in *Native Son* is initially instigated by a black against whites; in the other book, the assault is always directed by whites at blacks. Certainly *Native Son* is the much grimmer work, for *The Long Dream* contains some light moments—young Fish playing with a used prophylactic on a broomstick and dropping a loaf of bread for his mother into manure. Although Wright may present a more balanced portrait of black life in *The Long Dream* than he did in his earlier, more urgent, more desperate novel, the reader feels that he knows Bigger more intimately than he does Fishbelly. Even if viewed as a prelusion to "Island of Hallucinations," *The Long Dream* remains pretty much a rehash of the same ideas that Wright had developed more impressively in his earlier work.

By 1958, when *The Long Dream* appeared, Wright was feeling several tensions in his life. He was depressed by a lack of unanimous acceptance of the books he had been publishing; life in France had become as much of a strain as the one in America had been; and he had strong doubts about the quality of the book on which he was working, "Island of Hallucinations." When Wright's literary agent, Paul Reynolds, assessed the book, he did so negatively:

> [He] showed no enthusiasm for the novel. . . . He was sorry that Fishbelly had become essentially a spectator of the action, reacting mostly to overly philosophical speeches from his mentors. He also thought that the racial atmosphere of the United States had changed to such an extent [by 1959] that the references to lynching and other practices in the process of disappearing no longer rang true. Wright did not attempt to justify himself . . . , but merely explained that even if a sociological reality disappears, its profound psychological effects still remain, which was precisely the meaning of the book. (*Quest*, 484)

Of "Island of Hallucinations" only a portion entitled "Five Episodes" has been published to date.[7] In the first excerpt, Fishbelly can finally unbend a little after leaving America: " 'I've been toting a hundred-pound sack of potatoes on my back all my life and it's goddamned good to get rid of it,' he told himself" (141). He is, however, self-deceived; he cannot remove the weight from his back because his problems are caused more by the mind than by place. So inevitably, soon upon arrival, "exiled, he lived on his silent island [of hallucinations] moping about cafes, speaking only to waiters. Fishbelly was crushed, scared, lost" (141). In Paris, he still accepts white esthetic values when he undergoes all the trouble involved in wearing his hair in a conk. Like Jake Jackson in *Lawd Today*, Fish embraces values that are as shallow as those of the European and American middle class; for, worried about his appearance, he thinks, "Who could contest his stylishness? Did he not embody civilization, the advertisements in all the big magazines?" (142).

One day after leaving his hotel, Fish encounters a political demonstration; the crowd becomes mesmerized by his hat, which is decorated with a speckled orange-and-black band and a blazing red feather. Unfortunately, Fish's responses seem to be permanently shaped by his experience in America; for, when the crowd, chanting, " 'Quel Chapeau,' " follows him, he reacts as if he were being chased by a lynch mob because he does not understand the French language. After he runs back to his hotel, Mme. Couteau, the proprietress, and Mickey, the night porter, reassure him that all the crowd wants is his outlandish hat. Although Fish is having as much trouble adjusting to Paris as he had living in Clintonville, his maladjustment in France has results which are sometimes humorous rather than violent.

Episode II also offers additional qualification to the common view that Wright is humorless. Entering the restaurant operated by the Imbert family, Fish has to wait for a table because an old woman refuses to vacate hers. When she fidgets in her chair while looking for something on the floor, Fish again makes an assumption that does not obtain: he thinks that the old woman is racially prejudiced and therefore remains at her table to prevent his eating, even though she is finished with her lunch. Because the old lady still refuses to leave, maintaining Mme. Imbert did not give her her change, M. Imbert storms into his restaurant and insists that she leave. He forces her to go, but she creeps to the front window and peers forlornly at her table that is now occupied by Fish.

When he begins eating, he notices "a ghostly, disembodied, Cheshire Cat-like grin glaring up at him" (147); for the pathetic old lady has misplaced her false teeth. Out of compassion, Fish goes to some trouble to locate her and return the teeth: "She stepped close to Fishbelly, then paused in indecision; next came an abruptly brutal gesture; she snatched the laughing teeth with her left hand, and with her right sent a stinging slap against his mouth" (148). He understands the shame that caused the slap, for he himself had experienced comparable shame many times in

Mississippi. Shame, racial or dental, is the same in Clintonville and Paris. Fish never eats at Imbert's again.

The next three episodes are all concerned with showing that émigré blacks can be as exasperating a group as the southern blacks Wright was so happy to leave. They are variously superstitious, vice-ridden, and parasitical upon whites instead of being proudly independent. The character Ned, who appears in all three episodes with Fishbelly, is a protagonist in the narrative and a spokesman for Wright. Though he attempts fruitlessly to organize American blacks in Paris, Ned is thwarted because they have brought the debasement of their American experience with them overseas (*Quest*, 484).

The fact that Wright's usual grimness remains in abeyance in Episode III is illustrated by an incident that occurs when Fish and Ned are sitting at a table and the black nationalist Woodie sits down with them in order to give a disquisition about black nationalism. When he tells Fish and Ned that the ancient Egyptians were black, Fish interrupts:

> "So what?" Fishbelly cut jeeringly at Woodie. "Suppose the Egyptians *were* black, what does that get you? Soon's a nigger gets a little education, he gets sick of being black and he buys a big bucket of tar and a brush and he starts back in the Garden of Eden and slaps that tarbrush on God's face, Adam's face, Eve's face, Moses' face, and right on down to Jesus Christ's face. And when he gets through making all history black, what has he got but a bill to pay for the bucket, the tar, and the brush? After that, he hasn't got money enough to buy a pot to pee in." (150)

Wright had no tolerance for racial chauvinism, black or white.

Woodie also claims that he can tell the earth's gravitational pull is decreasing in strength because, when he walks, he can almost float. He contends that the whites are controlling the solar system by making a natural satellite come close to the earth, which explains the weakening of gravity. Ned explains to Fish that fear of American racism causes Woodie to talk wildly; that, although it is almost time for him to return to the United States, he is not psychologically prepared to go.

In the subsequent, penultimate episode, Ned tells Fish about Irene Stout (who is thin), " 'the most successful American Negro woman in all Paris' " (155). Her racket is to write letters that are phony pleas for money and to send them to wealthy white Americans in Paris. Ned, happening to have one letter with him, shows it to Fishbelly, who sees that it contains a cynical appeal to a white sense of racial superiority: "I'm asking a good white man to help a good old colored woman who had done lost her way to get back home" (156). Wright's tendency to be ponderously didactic is sometimes evident even when he tries to be humorous. Although some easily gulled whites could have been deceived by Irene Stout's ruse, her attempted deception would probably have had to be a little more subtle than her extremely obvious strategy of racial exploitation.

Episode V, the last, is Ned's narration to Fish of the history of the " 'streamlined, twentieth-century pimp' " (158) Jimmy Whitfield, who is " 'a sexual technician, limiting his own practice to frigid white women' " (160). An example of Cleaver's Supermasculine Menial, Jimmy is " 'redeeming his blighted racial pride by inflicting upon the womanhood of the race that had scorned him that part of his body that that race had condemned' " (161). His sexual exploitation succeeds until he turns from older women to a young one of wealth and social position. One day, when his new girlfriend is absent, Jimmy steals from her; but, since the young woman loves him, she drops her legal charges against him; and the police release him from jail. He then returns to a former mistress, the wife of a steel magnate, who wants him back if he will marry her. He agrees, makes her pregnant to insure the bargain, and leaves with her for France. Upon hearing about Jimmy's liaison, the rich young woman informs the French embassy in America that he is a criminal. After the French embassy sends the report to France, Jimmy is given twenty-four hours to leave the country, even though he is now the father of a French baby boy.

When Jimmy turns to Ned, the story's narrator, for help, Ned's plan is for Jimmy to break the law in order to get legal protection. After Jimmy has smashed a jewelry store window in order to be arrested and is under custody, his imminent exportation is made public; racial organizations come to his aid; he is given a card of identity. Like Bigger Thomas and Big Boy, he is invisible until he becomes a criminal; but, in Jimmy's case, the irony is that gaining visibility is salvation because it insures his stay in France. After he tires of the steel magnate's ex-wife, he returns to fleecing young girls; and Jimmy's business success is certain to continue for as long as he is willing to define himself as a black phallus that ministers to white sexual repression.

CHAPTER 5

An Exile's Nonfiction

I *Africa*

WRIGHT'S visit to Ghana (then called the Gold Coast) in 1953 led to his writing *Black Power* (1954), in which he regained his stylistic competence. Although *Savage Holiday* and *The Outsider* often succumb to vague, abstract diction, the syntax and the vocabulary in *Black Power* are under such tight control that they are reminiscent of *Black Boy*. In the preface, "Apropos of Prepossessions," he warns the reader about one facet of his *modus operandi*: that his twelve-year membership (from 1933 to 1944) in the Communist party was still heavy on his mind. He claims, "My relinquishing of membership in that party was not dictated by outside pressure or interest; it was caused by my conviction that Marxist Communism, though it was changing the world, was changing the world in a manner that granted me even less freedom than I had possessed before."[1] He then announces that "the aim of this book is to pose this problem [communism versus the West] anew in an area of the world where the issue has not been decided, an area that is proving a decisive example for an entire continent" (xiii). Despite his stance as a foe of communism, he clearly retained Marxist sympathies, and that retention causes him a major difficulty in judging Ghana. In *Native Son*, he had viewed social dislocation as a function of class struggle and/or racial struggle; and he brought the same quasi-Marxist perceptual grid to Ghana where only one race exists and where the industrial proletariat is not yet born.

Another, even greater, intellectual liability that Wright took with him to Ghana was the fact that he was an intellectual Westerner rather than a spiritual descendant of Africa. The reader wishes he had been more critical of Western assumptions, for

Black Power is sometimes too reminiscent of Booker T. Washington's accommodationist *Up From Slavery*: the Africans must become detribalized, industrialized, and technologically oriented. As in *Black Boy*, Wright does not give the indigenous culture enough credit; and it does not seem to occur to him that tribal culture may have a great deal worthy of retention. His predilection for Americanization leads him to decide that "the West can meanly lose Africa, or the West can nobly save Africa" (xv). But the notion that the West might bring about the secular redemption of black Africa is condescending to the Africans, who would presumably prefer to "save" themselves. Although Wright avows objectivity about different cultures, he persistently reveals his ethnocentric assumption that Western technology is superior to the African oral, tribal culture.

Part One, "Approaching Africa," shows him maintaining his environmentalism in regard to racial differences. In response to a cultural nationalist's claim that blacks have a " '*special* gift for music, dancing, rhythm and movement,' " Wright replies, "to me talk of that sort had always seemed beside the point; I had always taken for granted the humanity of Africans as well as that of other people. And being either uninterested or unable to accept such arguments, I'd always remained silent in such conversations. My kind of thinking was impotent when it came to explaining life in 'racial' terms" (5-6). To Wright, all men dip into the same undifferentiated genetic pool; and cultural characteristics are a matter of social conditioning rather than of some mystical racial difference.

His environmentalism also causes him to reject the "African Survivals" hypothesis of the anthropologist Melville Herskovits and his supporters who claim that much of American black culture is determined by earlier and only unconsciously remembered African ways of the first generations of slaves. Like the sociologist E. Franklin Frazier, Wright's faith in environmental explanations is nearly infinite; for he feels that "what the anthropologists have been trying to explain are not 'African survivals' at all—they are but the retention of basic and primal attitudes toward life." This extreme oversimplification is characteristic of Wright's approach in *Black Power*; the reader feels instinctively that Wright's thesis is undercut by his own example: "I'd seen these same snakelike, veering dances before. . . . Where? Oh,

God, yes; in America, in storefront churches, in Holy Roller Tabernacles, on the plantations of the Deep South" (56).

An adumbration of one of Wright's subsequent books, *Pagan Spain*, which is concerned with Protestant "outsiderness" in an oppressively Catholic country, also appears in Part One of *Black Power*. When Wright and his acquaintance Justice Thomas, who is on the Supreme Court of Nigeria, visit a house of prostitution during a stopover on the Canary Islands, Wright says, "It occurred to me that this shabby whorehouse was perhaps the only calm and human spot in this strongly entrenched Catholic city of Las Palmas where Franco's Fascism was in blatant evidence on so many billboards." (24).

Meeting some African students, whom he refers to as the world's outsiders, he declares, "The foremost conviction I found in them—or maybe you'd call it mood—was that nobody should strive for a unique or individual destiny. . . . The historic events of the past forty years had made them feel that the only road into the future lay in collective action, that organized masses constituted the only true instrument of freedom" (28). Wright was ambivalent about the power of the individual to shape himself or to shape events. Since the Ghanians have always lived in a closely ordered tribal environment, they, like Bigger Thomas and Big Boy, have many strictures upon their freedom. Although their resultant attitude cuts against the grain of the implacably individualistic Wright, he may have accepted it as necessary in order to eventually generate opportunities for individualism. He felt that only when some "give" between individualism and culture exists could meaningful action be possible, for too many cultural impediments to freedom result in the bondage of Bigger Thomas and the superstitious members of African tribes, and too great an opportunity for individualism results in the atrocities committed by Cross Damon.

Upon Wright's arrival in Ghana, he is met by Mr. Ansah, a friend of Kwame Nkrumah, the prime minister. Some bitterness is painfully apparent when Mr. Ansah takes Wright to a store where some sales clerks inquire from what part of Africa his ancestors came, and Wright answers; " 'You fellows who sold us and the white men who bought us didn't keep any records' " (35)—this reply sounds like what the usually polite Wright wishes he had said rather than what he really did say; and such a quip also jars the usually well-modulated tone which is a major factor in making *Black Power* the best-written book of his Third World nonfiction.

Wright's preoccupation with human sexuality, which is even more conspicuous later in *Pagan Spain*, also manifests itself in *Black Power*, and his tendency toward hasty generalizations about it is embarrassing: "Undoubtedly these people had, through experiences that had constituted a kind of trial and error, and in response to needs that were alien to me, chosen some aspect of their lives other than sex upon which to concentrate their passions" (40). This hypothesis is confidently tendered to explain the seminakedness of the women. If Wright's prudishness is evident in his sexual anthropology, his squeamishness shows elsewhere: he is irritated by the drainage ditches in which urine runs and by the pidgin English: he is less an outsider in the West than he consciously realizes. The bourgeois values he eschewed in *Black Boy* are everywhere present in *Black Power*. Even matters of aesthetics give him away: "Though scarring the cheeks was being done less and less, it still occurred among the more backward [*sic*] elements of the population" (40).

The generalizations he makes about "the African" are testy and unacceptable: "I found the African an oblique, a hard-to-know man who seemed to take a childish pride in trying to create a state of bewilderment in the minds of strangers" (85). "I found that the African almost invariably underestimated the person with whom he was dealing; he always placed too much confidence in an evasive reply, thinking that if he denied something, then that something ceased to exist. It was childlike" (107). On the basis of a short time in *one* African country, Wright reaches such incredible conclusions that it is clear that "Africans were more alien to him than whites in America."[2] Baffled by much of what he saw, he substituted ready-made theories for empiricism.

The postscript to *Black Power*, written in the form of a letter to Kwame Nkrumah, is more of the same: "I found only one intangible but vitally important element in the heritage of tribal culture that militated against cohesiveness of action: African culture has not developed the personalities of the people to a degree that their egos are stout, hard, sharply defined; there is too much cloudiness that makes for lack of confidence, an absence of focus that renders that mentality incapable of grasping the work-aday world" (343).

Wright is certainly not diffident about offering his advice to emerging African nations, but the inevitable outcome is insult. Nevertheless, in *Black Power* he is still all too correct in his basic message when he warns the West that Africa is going to assert itself in any way it finds necessary to gain its autonomy and dignity. Wright, who is ingenuously proud of this political formulation, gives himself full credit as its original author; but he is really echoing many writers. For one, W. E. B. DuBois said in 1903 in *The Souls of Black Folk* that the history of the twentieth century would be the history of the color line, the West against the Third World.

But in *Black Power* Wright does embroider upon the theme and make it his own. He identifies the West's early maraudings, now lodged permanently in the part of the African brain that perceives global reality, as the root of the struggle between that "dark" continent and its pale exploiters. The West, whenever it could, destroyed the preindividualist cultures of the non-West, leaving in its wake of rapacity either nonsocieties or, sometimes, ghastly pretenses of what had been—because in the destruction of authentic culture, which led so surely to philosophic and economic manipulation, colonial imperialism waxed strong. But then, its maw glutted with whatever resources it chose, be they human or gleaned from the earth, the West withdrew, indifferent, leaving Nothing for the remaining Africans. Such a continental stage is set to perfection for the incursion of international Communism, which cloyingly promises a ready-made world-view, economic well-being, and freedom—without demanding (or, indeed, allowing) the concomitant leap to individualism. Wright saw Ghana as a paradigmatic example of this process of Communist seduction; for Kwame Nkrumah, its leftist leader, was trying to fuse tribalism with Marxist politics.

Wright sees, in short, a continental recapitulation of the American treatment of its blacks: the 350-year history of the black man in America is the history of black Africa for the last 2,000 years. Bigger Thomas has reappeared as the whole of Africa; the European-American West represents the Daltons and the Buckleys; the opportunistic Communists play themselves; and the essential relationship among those protagonists in both scenarios is identical. Wright's message to Africa is that it can combat the West's exploitation and yet avoid the specious "freedom" offered by communism if it will make the transition from an oral, tribal culture to an industrialized, individualistic, nationalistic one—and do so immediately. But he also alerts the West to the possibility that the continent's growth into maturity may less resemble Wright's ideal of rationalistic enlightenment than it does the stunted efflorescence of Bigger Thomas. This adjuration to society to take care that it creates healthy offspring and the concomitant warning to beware those whom it has arrested cruelly in their development, is central to Wright's work.

II *Asia*

The thesis from *Black Power* that is also the presiding idea of *The Color Curtain: A Report on the Bandung Conference* (1956) is that the poor and weak of the world are oppressed by tyrannical forces. In *The Color Curtain*, Wright has continued his metaphysical widening of the discussion of oppression. The basic focus of *Black Power* is, as its title suggests, the hoped-for escape of Africans from "negritude," from their blackness being the talisman that allows whites to exploit them. *The Color Curtain* displays the widened understanding that *any* "nonwhite" color will bring down white vituperation onto itself. Wright feels that his past of blackness in the Deep South makes him not only the perfect observer of deracinated tribe members in Africa but also an ideal reporter at a meeting of "the underdogs of the human race."[3]

The report is subdivided into five sections: "Bandung, Beyond Left and Right," "Race and Religion at Bandung," "Communism at Bandung," "Racial Shame at Bandung," "The Western World at Bandung." Wright devotes part of the first section to the West's response to a meeting of the world's "niggers." When one typical reaction is that of a young white American who preposterously inquires if the conference is not racism in reverse, Wright feels it is far from it; the meeting is merely an attempt to resist the racism so long inflicted upon it, to gather some small weapons to fight back. If, however, the Third World is persistently thwarted in such attempts, racism may indeed eventually thrive. The title of the first section, "Bandung: Beyond Left and Right," indicates that, in order to resist, the

Third World is willing to eschew political classifications in order to achieve autonomy and dignity.

Wright then describes the sadly preponderant white reaction to the brown and yellow people who are the hosts of the conference: "Even before leaving Paris, I was discovering how the reality of Eastern nations was reflected in many European minds: the islands of the Atlantic and Pacific, and the millions of people who lived on them, still meant spices" (18). In assessing those people, whole countries of them, as worthless or nonexistent except insofar as they have just one thing of interest to the West, spices, the West debases them just as it did the black slaves in an earlier day when it judged them exclusively by strength, job productivity, fecundity. Predictably, Wright finds that many Asians hate the West "with an absoluteness that no American Negro could ever master" (25).

Some of those oppressed members of the Third World—presumably those with strong, durable egos such as Wright's own—are able to combine their hatred of their oppressors with a meliorism that matches Wright's: "He [an Asian intellectual Wright interviewed in Europe before heading for the Conference] took the view that, in the long run, the impact of the West upon the East would undoubtedly be entered upon the credit side of the historical ledger. I was inclined to agree with him" (53). Wright has learned, in time, to deal so positively with his hatred, that he can even tolerate the destruction of metaphysical values of a people though the result is Nihilism. He apparently feels that the nullification is a temporary one and that the culturally subjugated country's vacuum can be filled in some way by such Western values as individualism, rationality, technology, science. He can even sound a little self-satisfied when he describes the West's cultural violation of the East:

> It was clear to me that the East held by the West as a fond image does not exist any more; indeed, the classical conception of the East is dead even for the Easterner. . . . He lives in his world, but he does not believe in it any longer; he holds on to its values with too much self-consciousness to live by them. In fact, his pretentious clinging to those old values signifies that he is trying to save face. This Pakistanian journalist knew in his heart that the West had been irrevocably triumphant in its destruction of his culture, but he insisted when he embraced a new way of life he was

going to do so on his own terms, with no monitoring or overlordship from Westerners. (70-71)

Wright either never realizes, or rejects, the notion that the secularization of the entire world by the West could result in a global acedia. And his applause for the westernization of the Third World is undoubtedly partially based on the same squeamishness about the practices of "backward" countries that he evinced in *Black Power.* In *The Color Curtain*, too, Wright apparently has a compulsion to report that he sees people defecating, urinating, bathing, brushing their teeth, and washing their clothes in a canal in Jakarta.

But he never wants the westernization of the Third World to bring along with it the development of the white man's racism; in fact, he is dismayed by a signal that the East is following the West all too readily in that direction. At the conference, Wright at one point receives his press card immediately while a white American journalist is forced to wait: the racial tables are squarely reversed. Rather than taking any delight in this turnabout racism, Wright is greatly disturbed: "Can the colored races, for the most part uneducated and filled with fear, forget so quickly the racist deeds of the white races as they strive to free themselves from the lingering vestiges of racial subjugation?" (115).

He finds yet another disturbing instance of Eastern mimicry of the worst of the white world in the existence of a new class of Indonesians who act like the imperialistic Dutch once did by exploiting the classes beneath them. But oppression, in moving from the white man's continent to the colored man's and in moving from white hands to yellow ones, has blurred, changed—racial despotism has transformed itself into the tyranny of yellow by yellow. Because a portion of one race has turned against the rest of itself, class structure in the countries has changed unpredictably. Ever retaining his Marxist sympathies, finding capitalist tyranny deplorable, and championing the oppressed races, Wright sees dislocations in Indonesia that upset his simplistic theories, that hopelessly blur his preexistent uncertainties as to whether class or race is *the* determining factor in society.

In the second section, "Race and Religion at Bandung," he points out how these two forces coalesced at the conference. Though he did not acknowledge the effect of his maternal grandmother's Seventh-Day Adventism on himself and though he did not recognize in other cultures the power of animistic, poetic orientations to cause secular changes, his own background probably did give him the ability to perceive the coalition of race and religion at the conference. He was essentially a nontheological Protestant writing about race; he instinctively realized that the black church, in its racialization of Christianity, is sustenance to Afro-Americans in their quest for survival. Just so he found that the Moslems (one of the largest religions of the oppressed area of the world) could use their strict, life-pervading religion to help themselves; for their dependency upon it caused them to reject one of the greatest menaces to Third-World freedom, communism. Wright pragmatically concludes that their religion, which he regards as even more benighted than the Christianity he has rejected, is something he can applaud because of the positive political consequences—the rejection of communism—that ensue from the embracing of Islam by the people.

The Communist Chinese leader Chou En-Lai, the presiding figure in the third part, "Communism at Bandung," knows that "the distance that separated Red China from the religious nations of Asia and Africa was great indeed" (158); and he shrewdly emphasizes the common ground between mainland China and the countries represented by the other delagates: " 'We Asian and African countries, China included, are all backward [*sic*] economically and culturally. Inasmuch as our Asian-African Conference does not exclude anybody, why couldn't we ourselves understand each other and enter into friendly cooperation?' " (159). Wright always perceives communists as eager to expand their influence and as often subtle and proficient at doing so. Wright asserts in this third section that the world is quickly becoming westernized in general and Americanized in particular: "A strange and new religion is in the hearts of these new Asian and African nationals. They feel that if they do not become quickly modern, if they do not measure up to the West almost overnight, they will be swallowed up again in what they feel to be slavery" (173). The communists, gladdened by these dislocations, speak sweetly at the conference—and wait patiently.

In the penultimate section, which deals with racial shame at Bandung, America's treatment of its black population is introduced by Congressman Adam Clayton Powell, the important black politician from Harlem: "With the exception of Congressman Powell, no delegates or observers at Bandung raised the Negro problem in the United States—a problem which is child's play compared to the naked racial tensions gripping Asia and Africa" (178). The people of the world with nonwhite complexions have had the tensions engendered in them by imperialists who force them to fixate on their color. They have become intensely, morbidly, self-destructively sensitive to it. No less a luminary than Prime Minister Jawaharlal Nehru of India tells Wright that "race feeling is in these people, and if the West keeps pressuring them, they will create racism in them" (179). Wright envisions an apocalyptic finale to racial self-consciousness, racial shame:

> Rendered masochistic by a too long Western dominance, carrying a hated burden of oversensitive racial feelings, he [the man of "color"] now rushes forward psychologically to embrace the worst that the West can do to him, and he feels it natural that the West should threaten him with atom or hydrogen bombs. In this manner he accepts the dreaded bombing long before it comes, if ever. Europeans told me that if an atom or hydrogen bomb ever fell on Asian soil from Western planes, every white man, woman, and child in sight would be slain within twenty-four hours. (193)

Wright's greatest sympathy for these humiliated colored peoples is for the Eurasians, the half-breed buffer zones between the egos of the white men and the emergent egos of the native peoples. In them no anger or egotism has emerged to efface the blight of their pallid, though definite, color. And ever free from racism, Wright also pities the sensitive whites who are forced by the system in which they live to hurt their nonwhite fellows—it is perhaps the perceptive whites who must bear the greatest share of all of racial disgrace.

In the fifth and last division, concerned with the Western world at Bandung, Wright acknowledges the dominating influence of the Western culture that the conference was supposedly called to reject: "the strident moral strictures against the Western world preached at Bandung were uttered in the language [English] of the cultures that the delegates were denouncing!" (200). Wright's parting advice to the West might seem neocolonialist: "Is this secular, rational base of thought and feeling in the Western world broad and secure enough to warrant the West's assuming the moral right to interfere *sans* narrow, selfish political motives? My answer is, Yes" (219). Although he is really more deeply rooted in Western assumptions than he realizes, he persistently views himself as an outsider. He feels it would be easier to deal with a rationalized, industrialized Third World, but the Western reader must recall the relationship between France and Germany in the last hundred years and be sceptical about Wright's claim. Even more strabismic is his mindless notion of the East and West as potentially monolithic antagonists, for such a premise overlooks too many internal disputes.

III *Spain*

Predictably, Wright's impressions of Spain in *Pagan Spain* show that he viewed another culture as a variation on the Bottom South. To him, Spain was, on the one hand, as alien as Ghana or Indonesia and yet it was, on the other, as familiar as Mississippi. Divided into four parts, this piece of journalism opens with a section entitled "Life After Death"—a title that suggests what existence is like in the post-Civil War Spain in which freedom is no longer a possibility and religion is freedom's deluding surrogate:

> The only thing that stood between me and a Spain that beckoned as much as it repelled was a state of mind. God knows, totalitarian governments and ways of life were no mystery to me. I had been born under an absolutistic racist regime in Mississippi; I had lived and worked for twelve years under the political dictatorship of the Communist Party of the United States; and I had spent a year of my life under the police terror of Perón in Buenos Aires. So why avoid the reality of life under Franco? What was I scared of?[4]

The tendentious, preachy, stuffed-shirt quality of this passage obtains throughout the book, for Wright has a tendency to announce platitudes as if they were profoundly original. And his naive gravity and polemicism grate in an embarrassing way when he discusses the Spanish Catholic Church: he pompously asserts that that most Catholic of countries is still pagan since it has never heard the gentle message of Christ; and he is never worse than when he stiltedly, didactically lectures a fellow visitor to the shrine on the true, heathen origins of the Black Virgin of Montserrat. His anti-Catholicism, a direct relative of his anticommunism and of his proindividualism, naturally predisposes him to find Spain morally unacceptable.

In the second section, "Death and Exaltation," the reader is informed that single women in Spain are treated like "niggers"; they are fair game for the sex-obsessed Spanish men and little more. And in the subsequent part, "The Underground Christ," he sees that Protestants are also "niggers": "What drew my attention to the emotional plight of the Protestants was the undeniable and uncanny psychological affinities that they held in common with American Negroes, Jews, and other oppressed minorities. It is another proof, if any is needed today, that the main and decisive aspects of human reactions are conditional and not inborn" (138). In this third nonfictional book, he has enlarged the sphere of the world's outsiders to include people who are persecuted not because of color, but for religious beliefs or gender. Though the move toward sexual equality of the 1960s and 1970s has made Wright appear less than profeminist in his incessant use of "manhood" to mean "self-respect," "integrity," or "courage"—a person of a more modern orientation toward the sexes would prefer "humanity" or "personhood" to symbolize those brave traits—Wright nonetheless severely indicts in *Pagan Spain* the culture that devalues and degrades men *and* women.

Although the last two sections are as tendentious as the first three, part four, "Sex, Flamenco, and Prostitution," does contain an episode which gives another glimpse of the sense of humor that Wright only rarely troubles to reveal. At a party given for him by three single women, he pretends to be a bull, charges one of the ladies, and "gores" her in the pelvis. His humor, though perhaps not either sophisticated or ironic, was very much a part of him; but he invariably uses it as a speculative springboard. His butting the virgin's groin with his head has thoroughly mortified her—he ruefully wonders if, in this country of sexual repression, he is beholden to marry the embarrassed woman; and he reflects sadly upon what environmental strictures could evince such a debasedly ashamed response to such salutary and mild sexual play.

This section includes much evidence of his obsessive generalizing about sexuality, a preoccupation noted also in *Black Power.* He theorizes that sexuality is like a balloon, round and wholesome naturally, that must, if it is squeezed, lose its normal shape and pop out somewhere away from the pressure. The church that represses the society causes men to scorn women yet lust brutishly after them; it causes mothers to teach their daughters coquettishness as toddlers in order that they can feign what they are not expected to feel. The inordinately poor wages paid to women for honest labor force them to become prostitutes and, as such, to play out the fantasies of men who cannot fulfill themselves sexually with the women they love. He asserts that "being a woman in Spain means being mistress of all the tricks of sexual seduction and almost nothing else" (153). Later he remarks, "Spain seemed one vast brothel" (187). But since prostitution and Spanish wifehood are passionless enterprises, the healthy sexuality with which the Spanish woman is endowed that is no less than that of women of other countries must find an outlet—the beautiful flamenco dance is the soul of that passion. Since such reducing of a nation into phenomena of sexual displacement is not a common enterprise among observers of the human condition, Wright's observations may reveal as much about his imagination and his interests as they do about Spain.

Wright's discomfiture with Spain, which is not limited to its sexual proclivities, may also be partly explained by the limitation of the rights and the suppression of the humanity of much of its population; but his reaction must also be due, in part, to his culture-boundness. While realizing his Westernness, he does not seem aware that that quality will be the cause of some of these negatives as well as the percipient of other, preexistent ones. His ethnocentricity is what caused him to "[lie] in bed staring in the hot darkness, not wanting to accept how men lived their lives on this earth" (186). Spain was revolting to him because it is a police state in which machine-gun-carrying guards were a usual sight. His faith in the value of freedom was of a religious nature; consequently, where freedom was absent, he found hell.

IV *Warning*

Originating in a series of talks Wright gave in Europe during 1950-56, apparently because of his need for money,[5] *White Man, Listen!* (1957) consists of four lectures, three of which are about the struggle of the Third World to gain autonomy, and one of which concerns the Afro-American war for freedom in black literature. The essential Wrightian theme persists into one of his last books: he had an obsession for seeing that the position of blacks in the Deep South is only the situation of all the dark races, of all the oppressed, on a global scale.

Some whistling in the dark about his own reactions as one of these outsiders appears in his introduction:

> I feel constrained, however, to ask the reader to consider and remember my background. I'm a rootless man. . . . Personally, I do not hanker after, and seem not to need, as many emotional attachments, sustaining roots, or idealistic allegiances as most people. I declare unabashedly that I like and even cherish the state of abandonment, of aloneness; it does not even bother me. . . . I can make myself at home almost anywhere on this earth and can, if I've a mind to and when I'm attracted to a landscape or a mood of life, easily sink myself into the most alien and widely differing environments. I must confess that this is no personal achievement of mine; this attitude was never striven for. . . . I've been shaped to this mental stance by the kind of experiences that I have fallen heir to. I say this neither in a tone of apology nor to persuade the reader in my ideological direction, but to give him a hinting clue as to why certain ideas and values appeal to me more than others, and why certain perspectives are stressed in these speeches.[6]

Actually, he never easily accommodated himself to any environment; he was neither at home in society nor in the universe; but he desperately wanted to be comfortable in both.

The first and longest of the four lectures, "The Psychological Reactions of Oppressed People," begins with some of the best expository prose that Wright ever wrote:

> Buttressed by their beliefs that their God had entrusted the earth into their keeping, drunk with power and possibility, waxing rich through trade in commodities, human and non-human, with awesome naval and merchant marines at their disposal, their countries filled with human

> debris anxious for any adventures, psychologically armed with new facts, white Western Christian civilization during the fourteenth, fifteenth, sixteenth and seventeenth centuries, with a long, slow, and bloody explosion, hurled itself upon the sprawling masses of colored humanity in Asia and Africa. (1)
>
> The West was no more conscious of what was taking place than the East; had the West been aware, the enslavement of the non-white races could have been accomplished in fifty years rather than in centuries. The European stumbled blindly, attracted to the rest of the globe by the powerful impulse to find a world that would permit free play for his repressed instincts. (3)

Wright then lists a number of reactions of oppressed peoples to their conquerors. Under an early rubric, "Who and what is a 'Savage,' " he says that a "savage" is the result of inept Western proselytizing; and, when he draws attention to the aural and visual similarity of "save" and "savage," he implies that they are ironically linked by cause and effect. A savage is a man who has lost faith in his traditional culture but has no surrogate for it other than the white man's religion, which does not suit his needs. The quasi-adopting of that religion will eventually leave him easy prey for the other "god" of the white man, technology, by which he may become enslaved.

The oppressed people are those with "frog perspectives": they are able only to look myopically up to the victors over them; they are unable to assess their own positions except to consider them as low and humble. Western man took care to define these other cultures as less than human in order to ensure his domination over them and to compensate for his own doubts of adequacy, to bolster his own feelings of humanness. The mutant he developed in the process is of course the "nigger," the inevitable product of oppression, regardless of the color of the oppressed. As a built-in stabilizer to the oppressor's ego-enlarging system, these oppressed have been stripped of the philosophic capacity—the uplifting concept of the unity of man has been hidden from them.

Wright feels that sentimentalization of "primitives" is another tool used by the West to effect domination; and he feels that such romanticization is not only harmful, but silly—he is as scornful of whites waxing enthusiastic about "backward" societies as D. H. Lawrence was about James Fenimore Cooper's delighting in

Indians when he had never seen the inside of a teepee. Wright feels that the Third World must shake off the characterizations it has been handed about itself and that it will have to industrialize and leave behind its old ways in order to avoid redomination. Unfortunately, he is so "intent on attacking tradition wherever he encounters it, [that] he cannot concede that cultural nationalism might play a constructive role in the 'independence struggle.' "[7]

Because the victimized peoples react to their victors by developing ruses to conceal their true feelings, they try to let Europeans see scenarios rather than their real lives. Wright insists that honesty and a lack of racial mystique are crucial to the emergence of the oppressed as global equals. To dramatize the racial insecurity of the Third World, to show the resultant inquisitiveness of Europe, and finally to convince that he himself has the answer to the problem, he describes a luncheon he had with an Englishman and a black West Indian social scientist:

> The Englishman kept asking me questions about Asians', Africans', and American Negroes' reactions to their plight, and I kept answering quite frankly. I noticed, as I talked, that the West Indian Negro social scientist kept glowering at me, shaking his head, showing acute evidence of something akin to anger. Finally he could contain himself no longer and he blurted out:
>
> "Wright, why are you revealing all our secrets?"
>
> Unwittingly, I had hurt that man. I had thought that we were three free, modern men who could talk openly. But, no. The West Indian Negro social scientist felt that I was revealing racial secrets to the white race.
>
> "Listen," I said, "the only secret in Asia and Africa and among oppressed people as a whole is that there is no secret."
>
> That did it. He threw up his hands in disgust and exclaimed:
>
> "You have now revealed the profoundest secret of all!" (18)

Perhaps partly because of his lack of formal education, he tends to announce clamorously in this first lecture ideas that are not novel. The habit of tendentiously "explaining" to straw men, or ponderously answering questions that would probably never have been posed to him, is by this fourth nonfictional book well-developed and tedious.

The second lecture, "Tradition and Industrialization," subtitled "The Historic Meaning of the Plight of the Tragic Elite in

Asia and Africa," is Wright's theorizing about the unwittingly good results that unconscionable Christian proselytizing has had on the Third World. Revolted by religious belief, which he considers to be a mental problem or, at best, a mental predisposition that must be overcome by any man of rationality, Wright contends that Christianity can be regarded favorably only in comparison with the mystical Eastern religious philosophies, which he finds even worse than Western belief. Speaking frankly if tactlessly, he avers that "I'm numbed and appalled when I know that millions of men in Asia and Africa assign more reality to their dead fathers than to the crying claims of their daily lives, poverty, political degradation, illness, ignorance, etc." (48)

He finds it ironically good that deluded missionaries brought their Christianity to the Third World—not because they were successful in their proselytizing, but because the message of Christ that they brought with them was so spectacularly unsuited to the Eastern mental cast that, in trying to shed their old beliefs for the seductive Western dogma, the "converts" lost the religious outlook altogether. A further irony of Western missionary work is that it has produced a Third World "elite" more "Western" (i.e., rationalistic and unreligious) than Westerners. Thus, "today, a *knowing* black, brown, or yellow man can say: 'Thank you, Mr. White Man, for freeing me from the rot of my irrational traditions and customs, though you are still the victim of your own irrational customs and traditions!' " (60). This elite group, tragic in that it has been roughly shorn of age-old predispositions and left denuded, is fortunate to have a cleansed, purged mind with which it can look dispassionately at its country's problems and governance. Wright concludes that this new elite must now be allowed to act upon its vision, even if it does so through the use of tactics with which the West is not comfortable. "THE WEST, IN ORDER TO KEEP BEING WESTERN, FREE, AND SOMEWHAT RATIONAL, MUST BE PREPARED TO ACCORD TO THE ELITE OF ASIA AND AFRICA A FREEDOM WHICH IT ITSELF NEVER PERMITTED IN ITS OWN DOMAIN. THE ASIAN AND AFRICAN ELITE MUST BE GIVEN ITS OWN HEAD!" (65).

Wright begins his third lecture in *White Man, Listen!*, "The Literature of the Negro in the United States," by pointing out that Alexandre Dumas and Alexander Pushkin were black writers who were at one with their respective French and Russian cultures, whereas only one black writer has been at one with America—Phillis Wheatley. But since Wheatley no black author in the United States has identified with the dominant values of the country because none has been allowed to do so. The crucial American value that the black writers have not been allowed to share, of course, is freedom. It is just this issue of freedom which is the central theme of Afro-American literature and distinguishes it from white writing in this country, which does not need to cry out for something its writers have at birth.

By 1900, Wright avers, "two tendencies became evident in Negro expression. I'll call the first tendency: The Narcissistic Level, and the second tendency I'll call: The Forms of Things Unknown, which consists of folk utterances, spirituals, blues, work songs, and folklore" (83). The first tendency designates middle-class blacks who wanted acceptance by white Americans but were denied it; Wright identified himself with the second tendency by quoting from his own "I Have Seen Black Hands" and "Between the World and Me." Then he concludes "The Literature of the Negro in the United States" by asserting that black literature as such will disappear when blacks are free. Writing by blacks is a kind of barometer of liberty for Afro-Americans, Wright contends, because the stronger the demand for freedom in their writing, the less of it they have; and, conversely, the more of it they have, the more muted the cry for it is in their writing. Wright summarizes this argument with his famous statement, "The Negro is America's metaphor" (72); he means that one can judge the status of freedom for all Americans, by considering its condition in the case of the black man in general and in that of the black writer in particular.

The fourth and final lecture, "The Miracle of Nationalism in the African Gold Coast," is a condensed version of *Black Power*. After Wright explains how Nkrumah and his followers transformed the Gold Coast from a British colony into the independent African state of Ghana, Wright is again betrayed by his Western predispositions: "Can the African get *Africanism* out of Africa? Can the African overcome his ancestor-worshipping attitudes and learn to doubt the evidence of his senses as Descartes taught the

Europeans to do, and master the techniques of science and develop a spirit of objectivity?" (133). He apparently assumes there is little worth retaining in African culture, and his recommendation for the continent is a near paradox: they should throw the West out and then become as Western as possible. Wright was trapped by the culture that rejected him into seeing the world in a way that denied non-Western values.

What he ultimately wanted was to see the world as larger than race, community, tribe, state. His attempt at positing a global community is admirable, but he seems to have omitted from his theory the necessity of a worldwide, mutual cultural regard that must exist before any unification can take place. The Community of Man can only be forged out of respectful treatment of all its disparate parts, out of acceptance of the sacred cultural values of *all* countries; and Western rationalism, so lovingly defended by Wright, cannot be the *sine qua non* by which all that is incompatible with it is rejected. *White Man, Listen!* is journalism from an idiosyncratic point of view, for the reporter's correspondence is preordained by his earliest experiences and by his lifelong commitment to intellectuality.

CHAPTER 6

Eight Men

I *Short Stories*

PUBLISHED posthumously in 1961, *Eight Men* is an anthology of five short stories, two radio plays, and an autobiographical essay; only the radio scripts had not been published before. The first selection, a short story entitled "The Man Who Was Almost a Man" (originally published in 1940), is graceful, quintessential Wright: it has all the themes characteristically associated with his early writing. A seventeen-year-old southern black youth, Dave Saunders, is frustrated in his attempts to gain recognition as a man; but, by purchasing a revolver for two dollars, he assumes that his manhood will be acknowledged. Aside from its obvious phallic significance, the pistol is an emblem of male strength in a wider sense; it represents power, mobility, respect. Like Bigger, Dave "accidentally" kills; he shoots the mule Jenny, who is owned by a white man. Although Dave does not know the psychological meaning of the accident, the killing of Jenny can be interpreted on one level as Dave's striking out at the oppressor by destroying his property; but, on a more provocative level, she represents that side of himself, his slave mentality, that he would like to blot out: he does not want to be a mule for the white man. At the conclusion, Dave boards a train to go Up South, where he foolishly imagines he can be a complete man. The Promised Land is a place where a man is not forced to be almost a man.

The subsequent selection, "The Man Who Lived Underground," is the longest, best-known, and most highly regarded piece in *Eight Men*. First published in several versions in the early 1940s, this narrative marks conspicuous changes in Wright's theme and manner: it advertises the change in direction he made after turning from *Native Son* to *The Outsider*. After having consistently coupled Naturalism and the exploration of racial experience, he now shifts to the Continental mode of using literature as a vehicle for philosophical speculation; he turns his attention to the larger subject of exclusion, and he also veers from Realism to embrace Surrealism and Expressionism. The literary antecedents of the story are Continental, as well. They are Fyodor Dostoevsky's *Notes from Underground* and Victor Hugo's *Les Misérables*, both concerned with outcast, underground men. Wright enlarges on their vision by including all humanity in the ranks of wretched, hidden, invisible men. His striking metaphor was no doubt appreciated by Ralph Ellison, whose subsequent *Invisible Man* is woven on the same theme.

Wright's man who lived underground is contemporary man, but he is no longer deluded by aboveground values. America is a sewer in which men wander blindly in the dark; but, in the case of Fred Daniels, the black protagonist, the paradox of the sightless seer obtains: he first "sees" when darkness obliterates his vision. Only when Fred literalizes the metaphor of his existence as an "underground man" by going down a manhole does he behold the truth—he is invisible, as are all men.

The underground man's first reaction to entering "the black depths"[1] is that "everything seemed strange and unreal under here. He stood in darkness for a long time, knee-deep in rustling water, musing" (23). By the end of his adventure, the world aboveground appears strikingly at odds with reality, and the sewer seems normal. Man's world drains moral trash from aboveground to hide it below. Fred Daniels, like the quester in Robert Browning's "*Childe Roland to the Dark Tower Came*," is an antihero who discovers the irrationality of humanity by leaving it; he even comes across a rat like Childe Roland (Roland says, "It may have been a water rat I speared,/But ugh! it sounded like a baby's shriek"). And, rather than thinking that he has heard a baby shriek, Daniels sees the "tiny nude body of a baby snagged by debris and half-submerged in water" (27). He comes to understand that America is a toilet.

He apperceives that America's institutions all lie just above the sewer line. Using his submerged invisibility to look through chinks in the floors of the buildings above him, he gains a metaphysical perspective on their occupants which is as novel and startling as is his vantage point. One embodiment of respectability after another is revealed: a church, an undertaker's, a movie, a meat market, a jewelry store. Dan McCall refers to this list as "a nightmare of recapitulation"[2] of black history. At the church, Daniels "felt that he was gazing upon something abysmally obscene, yet he could not bring himself to leave" (26). Daniel the seer-eschatologist of the Old Testament has been reincarnated. His vision occurs underground, in the dark, while aboveground those in the light are blind. The literal sewer may be beneath the surface, but the metaphorical one lies putridly above it.

Daniels's emotional dislocation grows apace with his shifting vision. After a while underground, he cannot remember what he has been running away from: like Franz Kafka's Joseph K. in *The Trial*, he feels he has done something dreadfully wrong, but what? "Though innocent, he felt guilty, condemned" (40). He begins stealing what the topside world values, not because he covets it but because he knows he can do so with impunity: "He did not feel that he was stealing, for the cleaver, the radio, the money, and the typewriter were all on the same level of value, all meant the same thing to him. They were the serious toys of the men who lived in the dead world of sunshine and rain he had left, the world that had condemned him, branded him guilty" (45). After "stealing" diamonds, rings, watches, and money, he plasters the last three items with glue to the walls of his cave and mashes the diamonds into the ground (Ellison appears to have borrowed this episode almost wholesale for the introduction to *Invisible Man*). Fred Daniels shares with Albert Camus's Meursault in *The Stranger* a lack of interest in social conventions; and, like Molloy in *Molloy* by Samuel Beckett, he cannot even remember before long his name.

The numbing shock of paradox (blind seer; the helpful, sheltering real sewer and the hellish, hostile, metaphorical one; valueless money) and unnerving jolt of oxymoron ("dark sunshine," "serious toys," "dead sunshine," "dark light") are the only furniture in Daniels's world of emotional estrangement. They underscore his nihilism: everything aboveground is worthless; public values are worthless; only he, the outsider, possesses nothing, which is all that is valuable. Fred Daniels then makes the same mistake Bigger Thomas does; for, having recognized his invisibility, he wants it to be seen: "He had triumphed over the world aboveground! He was free! If only people could see this! He wanted to run from this cave and tell his discovery to the world'' (50). Because he is utterly disoriented by so much freedom, he plunges back into a world described as "a wild forest filled with death,'' which recapitulates the metaphor in *Native Son* as exactly as Daniels reproduces Bigger's fatal plunge to visibility.

When Daniels finally reemerges, he moves in front of a car driven by a man who shouts, " 'You blind, you bastard?' '' (60); for in the upper world, the man with vision is sightless. Turning Plato's vision of the cave from *The Republic* on its head, Fred Daniels emerges from the dark enlightening bowels of the earth where truth lies to the dark, dazzling sunshine of illusion above. Dazed, gorged with his other world's absolute redemption, he decides that he must stop running because he has nothing in his absolute freedom that he need run from. Since he must advertise his message, which is not a verbal one but is his whole self—his liberating escape from blindness—he hopes to preach it at the church he had spied on from his chink; but, because of his reeking filth to which he, again like Molloy, is indifferent, the gathered faithful drive him away with abhorrence.

The congregation goes on singing the praises of the Lamb, whose message they claim to hear; but its present-day avatar stumbles to the police, who, the reader learns, have earlier in the day wrongfully accused Fred of murder and have then beaten a confession from him. It was to escape their prosecution that he ran underground; but now, after his epiphany of sewage, he cannot remember the policemen's names; he only dimly remembers his reason for flight. Going guilelessly to the policemen to confess his innocence, to share his happy message of nothingness, he wants them to know that, since absurdity is the condition of all men, all can be free; but the police, who do not understand, try to chase him away. When he finally convinces them to let him show them the manhole where he went underground, one of them shoots and mortally wounds him: " 'You've got to shoot his kind. They'd wreck things!' '' (74).

When the policemen push him, dying, back into the underground, he greets it happily in terms that evoke Samuel Taylor Coleridge's description of Kubla Khan's pleasure palace: "He felt the strong tide pushing him slowly into the middle of the sewer, turning him about. For a split second there hovered before his eyes the glittering cave, the shouting walls, and the laughing floor'' (74). The city's receptacle for its toilet wastes has claimed his body and his message of Existentialist deliverance. But Daniels has had the pleasure, denied to many, of finally "Going Home" —and to the only place in the world that accommodated him. Fred Daniels is a nonintellectual Cross Damon, a man who has reached behind all conventions, delusions, and pretensions and who has found himself and everything else to be nothing. But where Damon uses his freedom demonically, Daniels uses it mildly, tries to share it, and dies as a Lamb whose only resurrection is the beatitude of becoming one with the detritus of the sewer.

The story is a gloomy one, and the nihilism it exposes is an attitude that Wright had had ingrained into him in the Deep South—that existence is "a state of eternal anxiety" (55). But Wright now realizes it is a condition that obtains with all men. To be human is to be guilty, to be hopeless. In his review of *Eight Men*, James Baldwin makes the same point: "Wright's unrelentingly bleak landscape was not merely that of the Deep South, or of Chicago, but that of the human heart."[3]

The third section of *Eight Men* is "Big Black Good Man" (first published in 1957), which is perhaps the high point of Wright's small amount of humorous writing. Set in Copenhagen, the story is told from the viewpoint of a hotel's night porter, Olaf Jenson. The short (thirteen pages) narrative is Wright's bawdy coupling of two of the themes Eldridge Cleaver later made famous in his *Soul on Ice*, but Wright has reversed them, with great comic effect. As for the first adumbration of Cleaver's themes, it is immediately obvious that in "Big Black Good Man" the Omnipotent Administrator confronts the Supermasculine Menial; and their jobs are literalizations of their roles. The small, physically unimpressive Olaf's job is to administer to any and all needs of the hotel guests; the nameless enormous black guest is a sailor and a paradigm of potency; but Wright's Administrator, reversing Cleaver's description of his function, slaves basely for the Menial, who condescendingly rewards him for his favors. An additional theme, again Cleaver's in mirror image, also suggests itself. In the chapter from *Soul on Ice* entitled "Notes on a Native Son" (referring to James Baldwin), Cleaver says that the motivating force of Baldwin and of many other blacks is racial self-hatred, which engenders a racial death-wish. He contends that hatred of one's own dark color has as its counterpart the love of the white color of those who have given birth to the self-hatred. Only through mating with whites can the detested blackness be paled—and sexual longing for white flesh is born. A further surrender to the race that has become caretaker and conscience of the black race is the erotic love for white men by black homosexuals. In a black man's erotic attachment to whites who are men, he is doubly capitulating to power—to the most powerful race, to the most powerful sex. To Cleaver,

> The case of James Baldwin set aside for a moment, it seems that many of the Negro homosexuals, acquiescing in this racial death-wish, are outraged and frustrated because in their sickness they are unable to have a baby by a white man. The cross they have to bear is that, already bending over and touching their toes for the white man, the fruit of their miscegenation is not the little half-white offspring of their dreams but an increase in the unwinding of their nerves—though they redouble their efforts and intake of the white man's sperm.[4]

One first encounters white Olaf in circumstances that are perhaps heavy-handedly suggestive of the tale's looking-glass emphasis on the Cleaver theme of lust that is engendered by feelings of inferiority: "An inch of white ash tipped the end of his brown cigar and now and then he inserted the end of the stogie into his mouth and drew gently upon it, letting wisps of blue smoke eddy from the corners of his wide, thin lips" (75). Rapt in contemplation of his life, he muses that he is agriculturally successful, having grown the largest carrots of anybody the year before; but he remains wistfully childless. Intruding on his cigar-smoking and thoughts, there looms before him a "huge black thing" that fills his doorway: "It towered darkly some six and a half feet into the air, almost touching the ceiling, and its skin was so black that it had a bluish tint" (77). The black man is described in patently sexually suggestive languages: *bulging* chest; *rocklike, humped* shoulders; *threatening stone* of a stomach; legs as sturdy and stout as *telephone poles*. Olaf, at five feet seven, "scarcely reached the giant's shoulders and his frail body weighed less, perhaps, than one of the man's gigantic legs'' (77). He ''felt as though the man had come here expressly to remind him how puny, how tiny, and how weak and how white he was'' (78). The self-hating black that Cleaver describes could, in speaking of his emasculated role in society, repeat that last sentence verbatim by substituting only the word ''black'' for ''white'' in the sentence.

And Olaf follows through with that train of thought as surely as though he, not the self-despising black homosexual, had been the subject of Cleaver's essay. He bristles with ''anger and insult'' (79) when the black man asks for whiskey and a woman. ''He felt a deep and strange reluctance to phone any of the women whom he habitually sent to men. Yet he had promised. Could he lie and say that none was available? No, that sounded too fishy. The black giant sat on the bed, staring straight before him. Olaf moved quickly, pulling down the windowshades, taking the pink coverlet off the bed, nudging the giant with his elbow to make him move as he did so'' (80).

But Olaf relents, sends him a whore named Lena, and then spends the tensest, most upsetting evening of his life wondering about the couple's sexual gymnastics. He tells himself that the cause of his intense agitation is the thought of a white woman with a man quite *that* large, quite *that* black—for a smaller and paler person would be more suitable. Olaf would like the privileges of *prima notte*; the result would be his longed-for child. It is the unalloyed dark color that is sexually necessary to Olaf; he must periodically replenish his manhood with a more virile strain of sperm in the hope of conceiving. The spawn of that union, darker and larger than himself, is sufficient, he feels, for the needs of a white woman; for she has no manhood that needs energizing. When the whore leaves, he pruriently requests an accounting from her of the evening, and she testily replies, '' 'What the hell's that to you. . . . You wanna take over my work?' '' (81). Since Olaf has already procured for—''bent over and touched his toes'' for—the phallus of a hotel guest, he would indeed like to take her place.

Wright is earthily amused by Olaf's physical and racial intimidation which leads so surely to lust—and makes the inevitable ''tryst'' highly comic. The black man, after six pleasurable nights with Lena, approaches Olaf, blotting out all else in his vision.

Commanding Olaf to stand up, "the giant's black fingers softly, slowly encircled his throat while a horrible grin of delight broke out on his sooty face. . . . Olaf lost control of the reflexes of his body and he felt a hot stickiness flooding his underwear . . . hot wetness . . . was in his trousers" (84). He has expected his neck to be snapped and has discharged his semen *before* the anticipated severance of the spinal cord, one of the instantaneous effects of which is the reflex-action ejaculation of sperm. This premature orgasm confirms his worthlessness as a lover and ensures that the union will result in none of the longed-for offspring. Their love-making ends with Olaf's whimpering to his conqueror and with the big, black, and sexually astounding man's calling him "boy" in return for his troubles. The black man sails off, predictably leaving Olaf feeling vanquished, degraded, bitter, and vengeful. He is ridden with all the emotions of a man whose hatred of himself has compromised him.

Exactly a year later when the black man returns, "Olaf's thin lips parted and a silent moan, half a curse, escaped him" (86). The giant again encircles Olaf's white neck with his "long, black, snakelike fingers," and Olaf attempts to rescue some of his over-powered, diminished potency by going for a gun. But the giant has simply been measuring Olaf's neck in order to assure himself that the six lovely nylon shirts he has brought will fit him. The shirts, the only tangible outcome of their union, are white; none of their giver's coveted color is passed on to Olaf. The gift of clothing, a mistress's usual reward for sexual relationships, is ironically in thanks for the whore Lena's services on each of the six nights that he had spent with her. The neck measured and the shirts given, the black man zips up (his suitcase) and leaves the pathetic, laughing, crying Olaf, who, from the gift of the shirts, has concluded that his anonymous hero is a "big, black, good man." Olaf has suggestively reordered the normal position of the adjectives as surely as he would like to arrange "normal" sexual positions and orientation. When the giant tells him that he is leaving him to go to Lena, with whom he has kept in touch, his parting words to his inadequate, childless paramour are, " 'Daddy-O, drop dead' " (88).

Although this uncanny recapitulation of the same themes by two men, Cleaver and Wright, was not conscious, these two shrewd observers of the black condition, by independently formulating and tapping the implications of the idea, increased their stature as commentators on blackness in America and as individual observers of this little-mentioned phenomenon. Though their accounts tally in every particular, Cleaver reacts to his with didacticism, philosophy, mythicizing; but Wright, in turning a perversely natural black reaction on its head, makes it high comedy. The breadth and ribaldry of the piece's humor make it stand out as lagniappe in the corpus of a man who is usually grim, often prudish and squeamish.

"The Man Who Saw the Flood," the fourth selection in *Eight Men*, originally appeared as "Silt" in *New Masses* in 1937. It recalls "Down by the Riverside" in its concern for the endurance of a black folk threatened not only by the hostile natural forces but also by the crop-lien system of white capitalism. As in *Twelve Million Black Voices*, Wright is extremely sympathetic to the black family in this brief short story; without any bitterness, with stoic resignation, they begin life again after losing almost everything in a flood. The Socialist Realism here contrasts with the allegorical method in "The Man Who Lived Underground" and with the tongue-in-cheek of "Big Black Good Man" to reveal the extremes in Wright's literary strategies.

"The Man Who Killed a Shadow" (first published in 1946) is another variation on the Ultrafeminine, Supermasculine Menial theme in *Native Son* and "Big Black Good Man." Saul Saunders has spent his boyhood getting shuffled around from person to person, place to place, much as Wright did. He has emerged into adulthood alone (Saul-"sole"), solipsistic—fairly sure only of his own existence and dubious about all else. To Saul, the world of white people is especially unreal, shadowy, "an incomprehensible nothingness" (158). He works desultorily at a number of jobs, but the only one he finds stimulating is as an exterminator who is assigned to rat-killing: he recapitulates the beginning (and end) of Bigger's rise to infamy.

He then becomes a janitor in a cathedral where a librarian, nameless until the very last pages of the story, works in the church bookstore. She is "tiny, blonde, blue-eyed, weighing about 110 pounds, and standing about five feet three inches" (161). She complains to Saul's boss that he never cleans under her desk, and she insists one day that he do it:

> He went and stood before her and his mind protested against what his eyes saw, and then his senses leaped in wonder. She was sitting with her knees sprawled apart and her dress was drawn halfway up her legs. He looked from her round blue eyes to her white legs whose thighs thickened as they went to a V clothed in tight, sheer, pink panties; then he looked quickly again into her eyes. Her face was a beet red, but she sat very still, rigid, as though she was being impelled into an act which she did not want to perform but was being driven to perform. . . . Her legs were still spread wide and she was sitting as though about to spring upon him and throw her naked thighs about his body. (163)

Wright apparently wants to suggest that the repressed sexuality of the cathedral's librarian causes her to desire the Supermasculine Menial, who alone can trigger the mechanism of her orgasm. But that orgasm, for centuries considered a figurative death, leads Saul to circumstances comparable to those in which Bigger found himself in Mary Dalton's bedroom; for, when the librarian begins screaming, endangering Saul, he is forced to kill her. She remains as shadowy to him even as he murders her as she was when fully alive, and as little sexually attractive as a phantasm. When the inanimate *panties* that conceal her genitalia are described, there is sensuality in the description; but when the sex organs themselves of the once living woman are bared, he perceives them as an unemotively charged "groin" and does not even take a glance (166);—the sexy panties are then used to mop up her blood. Once again Wright characteristically inserts violence where sex and love ought to be.

Saul absent-mindedly pockets a "thin band of shimmering gold" from the corpse (165) and shambles off with the indifference one feels about the "murder" of a nonentity. When he is inevitably caught for the murder (his capture occurs while he is considering suicide—such an act would of course be redundant because, in having murdered a white woman, Saul is a "dead man"), he confesses the crime readily and, in so doing, has his first scintilla of belief in its reality as he remembers the horrible death-screams of the nameless woman. In the courtroom at the time of his death-sentence Saul finally becomes wholly aware of the substantiality of the woman he has murdered; and, in a Pirandelloesque twist, the reader is shocked at the same moment into the comprehension that the dead woman must ever remain a shadow and a source of open-ended bafflement.

Saul is mildly interested to learn that the corpse does indeed have a name—Maybelle Eva Houseman, a name richly suggestive of ripe springtime, of the flirtatious sexuality of a "belle," of womanliness, of housewifery. The judge confirms that she had worn a ring that had been removed from her, which the reader knows would be the plain gold band that Saul pocketed. Although the reader's assessment of the tiny blonde is nearly complete, she recedes into shadow as abruptly as she has left it for Saul when the judge states that she died a virgin (was she chastely, frustratedly married? feigning marriage [her boss early in the story calls her "crazy"]? a sexually disordered lay nun who works in the church's bookstore?) and that the girlishly named, sexually eager, virginal seductress was forty years old. The story's conclusion is an ironic echo of the ring that legitimizes sexual love: "the decedent's hymen ring was intact" (170). Saul will be executed because of white sexual neuroses.

II *Radio Scripts*

Two works from *Eight Men* are previously unpublished scripts for radio plays in which there is no narration; both are dialogues exclusively. The first, "Man of All Work," is a farce with the serious undertone of the emasculation of the Supermasculine Menial which results in the genesis of an Amazon. Carl, the surnameless protagonist, because he has recently become unemployed, is forced to use trickery to continue making payments on his mortgage. A gentle "family man" who is as adept at the nurturing of his children as his wife is, he has had the profession of a cook: because of his obvious qualifications for the job, he decides to pose as a female domestic in order to earn wages; this plan is another form of "passing." His interview with the white family that he hopes will employ him recapitulates the unempirical brow-beatings that, in *Black Boy* and *Native Son*, masquerade as job interviews.

Carl-"Lucy," having "passed" the interview, as well as the sexual reassignment, assures his white mistress, Mrs. Fairchild, that she "won't have any trouble from" him (105). And indeed she does not; but, by the end of the day, she and her husband have given him a bellyfull: he has had to help the mistress bathe and dress; Mr. Fairchild has tried to sexually assault him; the distraught, jealous Mrs. Fairchild, responding to her husband's behavior in an action rife with suggestiveness, pumps a bullet into the servant's thigh.

A doctor, Mrs. Fairchild's brother, perceives Carl's sexual sham and discloses it to the family. This information helps Mr. Fairchild formulate an alibi for the shooting which reflects the absurdity of the masquerade. He intends gallantly to take the blame of the shooting onto himself with the explanation that "I was protecting white womanhood from a nigger rapist impersonating a woman!" (125). But Carl shrewdly convinces Fairchild that the safest strategy is for the white family instead to pay his hospital bills and give him $200 in hush money so that explanation will not be necessary. Through his cleverness, Carl is able to keep his house; but, at the end of the play, he remarks, "I was a woman for almost six hours and it almost killed me" (131). Wright felt that 350 years of passivity had almost killed black manhood and that the survival of it entailed cunning, the doing of many different kinds of works, and the playing of many different kinds of roles.

"Man of All Work" violates the usual pattern of Wright's fiction in that the black intruder (Bigger Thomas, Big Boy) into the inner sanctum of the white world is himself wounded, without harming or killing whites. But neither his being wounded by them nor the gentleness he evinces for children indicates that he is any less of a potential menace than those other interlopers. Wright's reference and allusion to the story of Little Red Riding Hood make it clear that Carl-"Lucy" is a black wolf in sheep's clothing and is, therefore, a threat to whites. When Lily, the Fairchilds' daughter, asks her mother if the new maid knows about Little Red Riding Hood, Carl-"Lucy's" response is, "Miss Lily, I know all about her" (106). The following exchange between the domestic and the little white girl echoes the dialogue in the nursery tale between the wolf and the child:

—Lucy, your arms are so big.
—Hunh?
—And there's so much hair on them.

—Ah, that's nothing.
—And you've got so many big muscles.
—Oh, that comes from washing and cleaning and cooking. Lifting heavy pots and pans.
—And your voice is not at all like Bertha's [the former domestic].
—What do you mean?
—Your voice is heavy, like a man's.
—Oh, that's just from singing so much, child.
—And you hold your cigarette in your mouth like Papa holds his, with one end dropping down.
—Hunh? Oh, that just because my hands are busy, child. (108)

The same white racism that causes Carl to be Lucy also causes him to be a black wolf who may eventually devour Lily, a naive white, who represents Little Red Riding Hood.

The other radio script, "Man, God Ain't Like That . . . ," dramatizes the disorientation that "westernization" brings to Black African tribal cultures. A fictionalized rendering of *Black Power* and a darkly humorous recapitulation of one of the contentions in *White Man, Listen!*, the narrative indicates that, ironically, savagery begins only when missionaries force tribesmen to attach haphazardly to their old notions, first, the rarefied, Western notion of Salvation and, next, the religious veneration of technology—the grafting onto primitive philosophies of these incomprehensible, but seductive, Occidental delights creates in the unfortunate proselytes a world view that is far too rickety to support humanistic growth. "Savagery" looks like it might well be the noun form of the verb "save"; and, in fact, savagery is the inevitable effect presented in Wright's radio script.

The story opens on a pair of racist white American émigrés to Paris, artist John Franklin and his wife, who are motoring through the "romantic" and "mysterious" (132) country of Ghana. When their car strikes a native, they refer to him contemptuously as one of "these baboons" (133); and he is, in fact, Babu, a "Christianized," gospel-singing tribesman who reacts with abashed delight that he should have the "luck" to be hit by a white man's car. He feels that he is fortunate because the accident enables him to get a close look at the white people, who, to him, resemble the red-bearded, blue-eyed, Sunday-school picture of "God" (whom he cannot keep straight from Christ). When they take him into their automobile to get him to the hospital, he feels honored to be riding in such a fine vehicle; but he is ashamed to be getting his blood all over it. As they ride on, his hymn-singing "blends with the jungle tom-toms" (135).

The linchpin with which he anchors the force-fed Christianity to his primitive, superstitious tribal orientation is the blood imagery of Christianity (in the Eucharist and, more potently, in the crucifixion-resurrection) which tallies beautifully with, and probably informs, his personal juju (a West African word meaning "fetish" or "charm"). Babu's juju is the belief that the spilling of blood brings good luck, perhaps since, in his opinion, his hero Christ's spilt blood brought Him great power. The power of the juju is confirmed in Babu's mind by the fact that he, having bled from his split skull all over the Franklin's car's fender and seat, is subsequently asked by them to return to Paris with them. They wish to take him with them because they are as eager as were seventeenth- and eighteenth-century Continentals for the sensation of a "blackamoor" servant.

In taking what they consider the quaint, primitive Noble Savage with them as a "boy" to Paris, they construct the same inducement to mayhem that the Daltons did by "generously" inviting Bigger into their service. They have a near-epiphany of the dangerous nature of their amusement when Babu offers chicken chops to them at dinner instead of their requested beefsteak. He explains that he has done so not out of insolence but because "Babu's head hit Massa's car. . . . Babu then buys chickens and cuts chickens' throats and let blood run to Babu's dead papa to say thanks to God. Babu bless Massa with blood" (138). He then adds quickly to this speech—which the Franklins have considered winsome—the statement, less charming and more hair-raising, that "sacrifice chicken good to eat" (138).

When they take him to Paris, the city overwhelms Babu with its cathedrals, public buildings, magnificent houses. Through a horrible conflation of Christianity and juju, he believes that the reason white men have such technological marvels and that blacks do not is because whites found out who God was (Jesus) and killed Him. After He rose from the dead, God, so Babu conceives, gave whites technological power as a reward for discovering Him. Clearly, Wright is dramatizing in this radio script what he had described in *White Man, Listen!*: how the West is able to mold Africans by adding Christianity to their old tribal ways. Because the Africans are left disoriented by the rape of their native culture, they are easily seduced by the West's other "big gun," technology, which, in time, eerily replaces bastardized Christianity in their minds as a religion itself.

Babu runs away from the Franklin family and goes "underground," as do so many of Wright's characters. He lives in movie houses, which he considers sacred places; and, when he sees a picture of Christ during his wanderings in the French capital, he sees that it looks exactly like John Franklin. When he returns to the Franklin home, John Franklin explains to him that he was merely the model for the portrait of Jesus; but Babu is certain his "massa" is fooling him and that Babu has really found the juju for the acquisition of technology, just as in his opinion whites had found it when they discovered God to be Jesus. Thinking that blacks will at last have the technology that the whites have, Babu beheads Franklin, and a grisly variation on the Bigger Thomas/Mary Dalton theme is presented. The result of Franklin's "wild idea" (139) to bring Babu to Paris is that the Franklins have indeed made him into a savage.

The French authorities, assuming Babu's admission of guilt in the murder of Franklin to be a delusion of a religious fanatic who thinks he has killed God, send Babu back to Africa, where he is "busy organizing a new religious cult" (154). The standard pattern of the black man's being inevitably killed for the violation of whites is altered by Wright in "Man, God Ain't Like That . . ." because Wright feels that taking the African out of Africa (either physically or emotionally), and causing him to change his patterns of thinking abruptly, because of white whim, will result in that black man's returning to the "dark" continent to proselytize, to mutate others as he has been mutated. Babu's safe passage home is a sly, ironic suggestion that the whites are creating their own enemies.

The similarity of Babu's name to Babo in Herman Melville's *Benito Cereno* is more than a mere echo. In Melville's story, Babo is the depraved African leader of a slave revolt against the Spanish crew of the *San Dominick*. Like "massa" John Franklin, the American captain (Amasa Delano, who boards the *San Dominick*) in Melville's story thinks the black man is innocent and harmless because he seems to be. There is even a parallel between the two works in regard to beheading: Captain Delano imagines for an instant that, while Babo is shaving Don Benito, the Spanish captain of the *San Dominick*, it looks as if a black headsman is about to behead a white man at the block. The most important parallel, however, is the prediction of racial nightmare; for, although Babu is not consumed with murderous hatred and Babo is, his being sent back to Africa, where he tries to convert tribal blacks to his own vision of technologized Christianity, portends a racial holocaust, just as Babo's depravity results in the near destruction of the Spanish crew of the *San Dominick*. It is difficult to resist the temptation of concluding that Wright was updating *Benito Cereno*.

III *Autobiography*

The concluding item in *Eight Men*, an autobiographical essay entitled "The Man Who Went to Chicago," is a continuation of *Black Boy*. This essay dramatizes Wright's smashing against despotic fact in several episodes: his job as a porter for a Jewish delicatessen, his work for several burial and insurance societies (black ones, of course), his experience at a relief station, and his work as an orderly at a hospital. All four experiences forced him to conclude that the North was an industrialized, urbanized version of Southern Hell. But he had left the South with the same vision that had propelled Ben Franklin, Horatio Alger, and Jay Gatsby in F. Scott Fitzgerald's *The Great Gatsby*—the American Dream of Success: "Like any other American, I dreamed of going into business and making money; I dreamed of working for a firm that would allow me to advance until I reached an important position" (174).

His first "important position" was as a porter for the Hoffmans, the Jewish delicatessen owners. On one occasion Mrs. Hoffman asked him to get a can of chicken a la king from a neighboring store; but, because he was unable to understand her, he memorized the separate sounds; and his request was, " 'Mrs. Hoffman wants a can Cheek Keeng Awr Lar Keeng' " (172). The bitter humor resulted from Mrs. Hoffman's thick accent, but

Wright assumed she did not take more trouble in explaining what she wanted because he was black: "I was persisting in reading my present environment in the light of my old one" (172).

Eventually, after numerous other humiliations, Wright asked himself: "What could I dream of that had the barest possibility of coming true? I could think of nothing. And, slowly, it was upon exactly that nothingness that my mind began to dwell, that constant sense of wanting without having, of being hated without reason. . . . I sensed that Negro life was a sprawling land of unconscious suffering, and there were but few Negroes who knew the meaning of their lives, who could tell their story" (174-75). Wright was one of those few.

After his job as a porter, he secured another one as a dishwasher in a new café where his tenure was notable for his dealings with the white waitresses and his observation of Tillie, the Finnish cook. The white waitresses were unimpressed by Wright and indifferent to his blackness, but he was impressed by them—by the utter banality of their lives: "All my life I had done nothing but feel and cultivate my feeling: all their lives they had done nothing but strive for petty goals, the trivial material prizes of American life" (179). He concluded from encountering the whites that "the essence of the irony of the plight of the Negro in America, to me, is that he is doomed to live in isolation, while those who condemn him seek the basest goals of any people on the face of the earth" (181). The Finnish cook was not remarkable for her empty life but for spitting into the food she prepared; Wright was afraid that reporting her act would cost him his job—he finally did so anyway, but he was not fired.

He next tried selling insurance policies and then went on relief. "The thought of selling insurance policies to ignorant Negroes disgusted" him (184), but economic pressure forced him to do so. Nonetheless, he traded premium payments for sexual favors from young black women who desperately desired to keep their policies in force. When he eventually had to accept public assistance, he observed at the relief station many other people who had nothing at stake in American society: "I sat looking at the beginnings of anarchy. To permit the birth of this new consciousness in these people was proof that those who ruled did not quite know what they were doing, assuming that they were trying to save themselves and their class" (190).

The last episode in "The Man Who Went to Chicago" is Wright's experience as an orderly at a medical research institute where he and the other blacks who worked there were, like Fred Daniels, restricted to the basement corridors. One of Wright's responsibilities was to assist in devocalizing dogs so that their howls would not disturb patients: "When the dogs came to, they would lift up their heads to the ceiling and gape in a soundless wail. The sight became lodged in my imagination as a symbol of silent suffering" (195). This treatment of animals, this silent suffering by them, was an emblem to Wright of America's treatment of the black segment of its population, which it considered nothing but dogs, and the pain that treatment inflicted.

The incident that made the strongest impression upon Wright at the hospital was a fight between two fellow orderlies who knocked cages of rats, mice, guinea pigs, and rabbits into a jumble. Terrified they would lose their jobs, the black orderlies put the animals back, helter skelter, into any convenient cage. Wright was indifferent to letting the doctors know that their experimental animals had been rearranged: "The hospital kept us four Negroes as though we were close kin to the animals we tended, huddled together down in the underworld corridors of the hospital, separated by a vast psychological distance from the significant processes of the rest of the hospital—just as America had kept us locked in the dark underworld of America for three hundred years—and we had made our own code of ethics, values, loyalty" (204).

CHAPTER 7

Conclusion

RICHARD Wright found that the meaning of life was in meaningless suffering. The reasons behind his suffering were racial, familial, educational, economic, and philosophical; no other highly regarded writer has ever had to break through so many restrictions. What Wright accomplished is a monument to the vitality and toughness of his ego; for, in conditions that would suppress or destroy other men, he made himself into one of the most important American writers of the century. While much of his work is undeniably weak and unsuccessful, three of his books, *Uncle Tom's Children*, *Native Son*, and *Black Boy*, will always be read. How he managed to write three such books, given his background, is hardly imaginable; because, though the Deep South should have destroyed him and was designed to do so, it created instead an author with a unique mastery of the subject of humanity's attempts, so often successful, to shatter its own.

Wright's great theme, which he expresses in varying levels of abstraction, is that the oppression of mankind causes the moral, psychological, and physical degradation of the tyrannical as well as that of the tyrannized. This thesis, admittedly not a pretty one, is resisted even today by white and nonwhite readers alike, because of its very correctness—its implications are too painful. How then was Wright, whose life was ever afflicted by the societal hatred of his race, his atheism, and his Marxist idealism, able to bore away to the philosophical essence of oppression and then present it with such urgent immediacy? It was his immense resilience, his will, his imaginative powers, and his ability to use literature as a bulwark against insupportable reality that permitted his insights and his artistry.

The species of oppression that Wright is unsurpassed at limning is, of course, racism, because it was that particular demon that so nearly annihilated him. His exorcism of the blight of racial prejudice was two-fold: he described the horrors that devolve upon blacks and whites alike from a warped description of his race; and he further militated against America's scorn of blackness by celebrating the beauty and strength of that spurned culture in his writings and, indeed, in his very existence—his success is eloquent testimony to the extreme toughness and endurance of the Afro-American tradition.

Wright is not only the virtual father of the post-World War II black novel, he is also the dominant precursor of the Black Renaissance of the 1960s: by rejecting the exotic Bohemianism of the Harlem Renaissance in favor of a literature gorged with authentic black experience, Wright gave to his recent literary descendants the legacy of a body of writing important not so much for technical innovation as for the presentation of themes now joyous, now gut-wrenching, but always genuinely, proudly black. And he bequeathed to all his readers a crudely powerful exhortation to look unflinchingly at his themes—and then beyond them, into the heart. Though he is perhaps not an author who appeals to the weak-spirited, it is undeniable that artistic greatness is the lot of this man who never wavered from his vision of the truth or compromised his integrity. Because of what he accomplished, to name a twentieth-century American writer of more urgency and moral power is difficult.

Notes and References

Chapter One

1. A sociological term referring to that stage in a culture's development before it is secure enough to allow strong individuals to emerge.
2. Michel Fabre, *The Unfinished Quest of Richard Wright*, trans. Isabel Barzun (New York, 1973), p. 7; hereafter cited in text as *Quest.*
3. Richard Wright, *Black Boy: A Record of Childhood and Youth* (New York, 1945; rpt. New York, 1966), p. 13; further references to this book appear in parentheses in the text.
4. See Thomas Knipp, ed., *Letters to Joe C. Brown* (Kent, Ohio, 1968). This unauthorized edition of Wright's letters proves that his memories of Jackson were not all bitter.
5. *Shadow and Act* (New York, 1964; rpt. New York, 1966), p. 140.
6. Richard Wright, "Superstition," *Abbott's Monthly Magazine* (April 1931): 45-47; 64-66; 72-73; further references to this story appear in parentheses in the text.
7. "I Have Seen Black Hands," *New Masses* 11 (June 26, 1934): 16.
8. "We of the Streets," *New Masses* 23 (April 13, 1937): 14.
9. "Hearst Headline Blues," *New Masses* 19 (May 12, 1936): 14.
10. "Red Leaves of Red Books," *New Masses* 15 (April 30, 1935): 6.
11. "Between the World and Me," in *Black Voices*, ed. Abraham Chapman (New York, 1968), pp. 437-38.
12. "I Tried to Be a Communist," *Atlantic Monthly* 159 (August 1944): 62.
13. Ibid., p. 69.
14. Ibid. (August 1944): 61-70; (September 1944): 48-56. In 1977 Harper published a book called *American Hunger*, which is the second section of *Black Boy*. Although nearly all of this book was published as articles in the 1940s, it does gather them together for the first time.
15. Richard Wright, *Twelve Million Black Voices: A Folk History of the Negro in the United States* (New York, 1941; rpt. New York, 1969), p. 59; further citations in the text.
16. *Black Boy*, p. 131.
17. See Keneth Kinnamon, *The Emergence of Richard Wright* (Urbana, Ill., 1972). Hereafter cited as *Emergence.*
18. Robert Bone, *Richard Wright* (Minneapolis, 1969), p. 15.

Chapter Two

1. George E. Kent, "Richard Wright: Blackness and the Adventure of Western Culture," *College Language Association Journal* 12 (June 1969): 335.
2. *Lawd Today* (New York, 1963), p. 8; further references to this novel are incorporated into the text in parentheses.
3. *Uncle Tom's Children* (New York, 1938, 1940; rpt. New York, 1965), p. 23; further references to this book are incorporated into the text in parentheses.
4. Dan McCall, *The Example of Richard Wright* (New York, 1969), p. 35. Hereafter cited as *Example*.
5. Keneth Kinnamon, *Emergence*, pp. 84-85.
6. Dan McCall, *Example*, p. 44.
7. Constance Webb, *Richard Wright* (New York, 1968), p. 402, n. 6.
8. Ibid., p. 137, n. 8.
9. *Example*, p. 33.
10. Ibid., pp. 33, 34.
11. But see Campbell Tatham, "Vision and Value in *Uncle Tom's Children*," *Studies in Black Literature* 3 (Spring 1972): 14-23. Tatham argues not very convincingly that the addition of "The Ethics of Living Jim Crow" and "Bright and Morning Star" to the 1940 edition was artistic.

Chapter Three

1. *Soul on Ice* (New York, 1968), p. 171. Further immediate references will be incorporated into the text in parentheses.
2. *Native Son* (New York, 1940; rpt. New York, 1966); p. 16; further references in the text.
3. Keneth Kinnamon, *Emergence*, p. 121.
4. "I Bite the Hand That Feeds Me," *Atlantic Monthly* 155 (June 1940): 828.
5. Darwin T. Turner, "*The Outsider*: Revision of an Idea," *College Language Association Journal* 12 (June 1969): 314.
6. Introduction to Nelson Algren, *Never Come Morning* (New York, 1942), p. x.
7. S. P. Fullinwider, *The Mind and Mood of Black America* (Homewood, Ill., 1969), p. 191.
8. See Paul N. Siegel, "The Conclusion of Richard Wright's *Native Son*," *Publications of the Modern Language Association* 89 (May 1974): 515-23.
9. Morris Weitz, *Philosophy of the Arts* (New York, 1964), p. 141.

10. Houston A. Baker, Jr., *Long Black Song* (Charlottesville, 1972), p. 127.
11. Ibid., p. 133.
12. Lance Jeffers, "Afro-American Literature, the Conscience of Man," *Black Scholar* 2 (January 1971): 50.
13. "I Bite the Hand That Feeds Me," p. 828.
14. David B. Gibson, "Richard Wright and the Tyranny of Convention," *College Language Association Journal* 12 (June 1969): 349, n. 2.
15. Morris Dickstein, "Wright, Baldwin, Cleaver," in *Richard Wright: Impressions and Perspectives*, ed. David Ray and Robert M. Farnsworth (Ann Arbor, 1973), p. 188.
16. Saunders Redding, "The Alien Land of Richard Wright," in *Five Black Writers*, ed. Donald B. Gibson (New York, 1970), pp. 5-6.
17. Keneth Kinnamon, *Emergence*, pp. 119, 143.
18. *Notes of a Native Son* (New York, 1963), p. 29.
19. Ibid., p. 22.
20. "The World and the Jug," in *Shadow and Act*, p. 119.
21. In *Five Black Writers*, pp. 12-25.

Chapter Four

1. Richard Wright, *The Outsider* (New York, 1953; rpt. New York, 1965), p. 3; further references in parentheses in the text.
2. Lewis A. Lawson, "Cross Damon: Kierkegaardian Man of Dread," *College Language Association Journal* 14 (March 1971): 305.
3. Arthur P. Davis, " 'The Outsider' as a Novel of Race," *Midwest Journal* 7 (Winter 1956): 320-26.
4. *Savage Holiday* (New York, 1954; rpt. New York, 1969), p. 11; further references in the text.
5. *Richard Wright*, p. 314.
6. *The Long Dream* (New York, 1958; rpt. Chatham, N. J., 1969), p. 24; further references in parentheses in the text.
7. Excerpts from "Island of Hallucinations" have appeared as "Five Episodes" in *Soon, One Morning*, ed. Herbert Hill (New York, 1963), pp. 140-64; citations in the text.

Chapter Five

1. *Black Power* (New York, 1954), p. xi; further references in parentheses in the text.
2. Constance Webb, *Richard Wright*, p. 334.
3. *The Color Curtain* (Cleveland and New York, 1956), p. 12; further references in parentheses in the text.

4. *Pagan Spain* (New York, 1956), p. 1; further references in parentheses in the text.
5. Webb, *Richard Wright*, p. 358.
6. *White Man, Listen!* (New York, 1957; rpt. Garden City, New York, 1964), pp. xvi-xvii; further references in parentheses in the text.
7. Bone, *Richard Wright*, p. 37.

Chapter Six

1. *Eight Men* (Cleveland and New York, 1961; rpt. New York, 1969), p. 22; further references in parentheses in the text. Fabre says Wright got the idea for the underground from a piece in *True Detective* (*Quest*, p. 574, n. 53).
2. *Example*, p. 169.
3. *Nobody Knows My Name* (New York, 1961; rpt. New York, 1969), p. 149.
4. *Soul on Ice*, p. 100.

Selected Bibliography

Primary Sources

"Superstition." *Abbott's Monthly Magazine* 2 (April 1931): 45-47, 64-66, 72-73.
"A Red Love Note." *Left Front* 3 (January-February 1934): 3.
"Rest for the Weary." *Left Front* 3 (January-February 1934): 3.
"I Have Seen Black Hands." *New Masses* 11 (June 26, 1934): 16.
"Red Leaves of Red Books." *New Masses* 15 (April 30, 1935): 6.
"Between the World and Me." *Partisan Review* 2 (July-August 1935): 18-19.
"Spread Your Sunrise." *New Masses* 16 (July 2, 1935): 26.
"Hearst Headline Blues." *New Masses* 19 (May 12, 1936): 14.
"We of the Streets." *New Masses* 23 (April 13, 1937): 14.
"The Ethics of Living Jim Crow." In *American Stuff* (Federal Writer's Project anthology). New York: 1937, pp. 39-52. Included in *Uncle Tom's Children* (1940 edition).
"Blueprint for Negro Writing." *New Challenge* 2 (Fall 1937): 53-65.
Uncle Tom's Children. New York: Harper, 1938. The 1940 edition adds "The Ethics of Living Jim Crow" and "Bright and Morning Star."
Native Son. New York: Harper, 1940.
"How 'Bigger' Was Born." New York: Harper, 1940. Included in the Harper Perennial Classic edition of *Native Son*.
"I Bite the Hand That Feeds Me." *Atlantic Monthly* 155 (June 1940): 826-28.
Native Son, the Biography of a Young American. A Play in Ten Scenes. New York: Harper, 1941. (Written in collaboration with Paul Green.)
Twelve Million Black Voices: A Folk History of the Negro in the United States. New York: Viking, 1941.
"What You Don't Know Won't Hurt You." *Harper's Magazine* 186 (December 1942): 58-61.
"Introduction." In Nelson Algren, *Never Come Morning*. New York: Harper, 1942, pp. ix-x.
"I Tried to Be a Communist." *Atlantic Monthly* 159 (August 1944): pp. 61-70; (September 1944): 48-56.
"Introduction." In Horace R. Cayton and St. Clair Drake, *Black Metropolis*. New York: Harcourt Brace, 1945, pp. xvii-xxxiv.

Black Boy. New York: Harper, 1945.
The Outsider. New York: Harper, 1953.
Savage Holiday. New York: Avon, 1954.
Black Power. New York: Harper, 1954.
The Color Curtain. Cleveland and New York: World Publishing Company, 1956.
Pagan Spain. New York: Harper, 1956.
White Man, Listen!. New York: Doubleday, 1957.
The Long Dream. New York: Doubleday, 1958.
Eight Men. Cleveland and New York: World Publishing Company, 1961.
Lawd Today. New York: Walker, 1963.
"Five Episodes." in *Soon, One Morning*. Ed. Herbert Hill. New York: Knopf, 1963, pp. 140-64. From "Island of Hallucinations."
American Hunger. New York: Harper, 1977.
Richard Wright Reader. Ed. Ellen Wright and Michel Fabre. New York: Harper, 1978.

SECONDARY SOURCES

ABCARIAN, RICHARD, ed. *Richard Wright's "Native Son": A Critical Handbook*. Belmont, Calif.: Wadsworth Publishing Co., 1970. Very useful compilation of material: essay by Wright, reviews of the novel, critical essays, chronology, bibliography.

BAKER, HOUSTON A., JR. *Long Black Song: Essays in Black American Literature and Culture*. Charlottesville: University Press of Virginia, 1972. Applies a black aesthetic to Wright.

———, ed. *Twentieth Century Interpretations of "Native Son."* Englewood Cliffs, N. J.: Prentice-Hall, Inc., 1972. Contains some of the best essays ever written about the novel.

BALDWIN, JAMES. "Alas, Poor Richard." In *Nobody Knows My Name*. New York: Dial Press, 1961. "It now begins to seem . . . that Wright's unrelentingly bleak landscape was not merely that of the Deep South, or of Chicago, but that of the world, of the human heart."

———. "Everybody's Protest Novel." *Zero* 1 (Spring 1949): 54-58. Frequently reprinted, centrally important: Bigger's tragedy is that "he has accepted a theology that denies him life."

———. "Many Thousands Gone." *Partisan Review* 18 (November-December 1951): 665-80. One of the most provocative essays ever written about Wright; frequently reprinted, most conveniently in *Notes of a Native Son* (New York, 1963), which also includes "Everybody's Protest Novel."

BONE, ROBERT A. *The Negro Novel in America*. Rev. ed. New Haven:

Yale University Press, 1965. Includes a substantial section on *Native Son*.

______. *Richard Wright*. Minneapolis: University of Minnesota Press, 1969. The best short critical study.

BRIGNANO, RUSSELL CARL. "Richard Wright: A Bibliography of Secondary Scources [*sic*]." *Studies in Black Literature* 2 (Summer 1971): 19-25. Very useful, although it does not include contemporary reviews.

______. *Richard Wright: An Introduction to the Man and His Works*. Pittsburgh: University of Pittsburgh Press, 1970. Summary of Wright's major ideas and themes.

BROWN, CECIL M. "Richard Wright: Complexes and Black Writing Today." *Negro Digest* 18 (December 1968): 45-50, 78-82. Attacks Wright for his negative protest; he is the Booker T. Washington of Afro-American letters. Reprinted in Abcarian.

BROWN, LLOYD W. "Stereotypes in Black and White: The Nature of Perception in Wright's *Native Son*." *Black Academy Review* 1 (Fall 1970): 35-44. "Bigger's spiritual liberation is more apparent than real." Very suggestive.

BRYER, JACKSON R. "Richard Wright (1908-1960): A Selected Checklist of Criticism," *Wisconsin Studies in Contemporary Literature* 1 (Fall 1960): 22-33. Still useful, especially because of its list of contemporary reviews.

CLEAVER, ELDRIDGE. "Notes on a Native Son." In *Soul on Ice*. New York: McGraw-Hill, 1967. Defense of Wright against Baldwin's assertions.

College Language Association Journal 12 (June 1969). Special Wright number. Contains Darwin Turner's article on *The Outsider*, cited herein, and a provocative article by Donald B. Gibson, "Richard Wright and the Tyranny of Convention."

DAVIS, ARTHUR P. " 'The Outsider' as a Novel of Race." *Midwest Journal* 7 (Winter 1956): 320-26. *The Outsider* as a new type of race novel.

DICKSTEIN, MORRIS. "Wright, Baldwin, Cleaver," *New Letters* 38 (1971): 117-24. Reprinted in Ray and Farnsworth (see Ray, below). Helps to explain the confusion between Bigger as reborn and Bigger as damned.

ELLISON, RALPH. "The World and the Jug." In *Shadow and Act*. New York: Random House, 1964. Ellison is at pains to deny Wright's influence on himself and the validity of Wright's picture of black life.

EMANUEL, JAMES A. "Fever and Feeling: Notes on the Imagery in *Native Son*." *Negro Digest* 18 (December 1968): 16-26. Suggestive essay about some of the image clusters.

FABRE, MICHEL. "The Poetry of Richard Wright." *Studies in Black Literature* 1 (Autumn 1970): 11-22. The most comprehensive study of Wright's poetry.

———. *The Unfinished Quest of Richard Wright*. Trans. Isabel Barzun. New York: William Morrow, 1973. May well come to be regarded as the definitive biography; contains much new information.

———, and MARGOLIES, EDWARD. "Richard Wright (1908-1960): A Bibliography." *Bulletin of Bibliography* 24 (January-April 1965): 131-33, 137. Reprinted in Fabre's biography in a revised and enlarged version.

FELGAR, ROBERT. " 'The Kingdom of the Beast': The Landscape of *Native Son*." *College Language Association Journal* 17 (March 1974): 333-37. Beast imagery as one of the novel's presiding metaphors.

———. "*Soul on Ice* and *Native Son*." *Negro American Literature Forum* (now *Black American Literature Forum*) 8 (Fall 1974): 235. Application of Cleaver's theory of sexuality to *Native Son*.

FISHBURN, KATHERINE. *Richard Wright's Hero: The Faces of a Rebel-Victim*. Metuchen, N. J.: Scarecrow Press, 1977. "Wright's archetypal hero is the rebel-victim who cries out for immediate universal justice."

FULLINWIDER, S. P. *The Mind and Mood of Black America*. Homewood, Ill.: Dorsey Press, 1969. The emptiness of black history reflected in *Native Son*.

GIBSON, DONALD B., ed. *Five Black Writers*. New York: New York University Press, 1970. Includes several of the best essays about Wright.

———. "Wright's Invisible Native Son." *American Quarterly* 21 (Winter 1969): 728-38. "The figure on the final pages of the novel, no matter what he is, is not a rat. He does not die as a rat dies; he is neither fearful nor desperate."

GRENANDER, M. E. "Criminal Responsibility in *Native Son* and *Knock on Any Door*." *American Literature* 49 (May 1977): 221-33. "Each novel ends by accepting the doctrine of criminal responsibility."

HILL, HERBERT, et al. "Reflections on Richard Wright: A Symposium of an Exiled Native Son." In *Anger, and Beyond: The Negro Writer in the United States*. Ed. Herbert Hill. New York: Harper, 1966, pp. 196-212. Reprinted in *Five Black Writers*. Contains numerous insights into Wright by men who knew him.

HOWE, IRVING. "Black Boys and Native Sons." *Dissent* 10 (Autumn 1963): 353-68. A defense of Wright against Baldwin. Crucial essay; frequently reprinted.

JEFFERS, LANCE. "Afro-American Literature, the Conscience of Man." *Black Scholar* 2 (January 1971): 47-53. Bigger is reborn in prison.

KINNAMON, KENETH. *The Emergence of Richard Wright*. Urbana: University of Illinois Press, 1972. Analysis of the environment Wright transformed into art.

MARGOLIES, EDWARD. *The Art of Richard Wright*. Carbondale: Southern Illinois University Press, 1969. General critical study.

______. *Native Sons: A Critical Study of Twentieth-Century Negro American Authors*. Philadelphia: J. B. Lippincott, 1968. Includes a section on three kinds of revolution in *Native Son*.

McCALL, DAN. *The Example of Richard Wright*. New York: Harcourt Brace, 1969. Contains some of the best criticism of "Big Boy Leaves Home" and *Native Son*, but the charge of plagiarism has been raised against it: see Keneth Kinnamon, "*The Example of Richard Wright* by Dan McCall," *Journal of English and Germanic Philology* 70 (January 1971): 180-86; (October 1971): 753-54.

Negro Digest (now *Black World*) 18 (December 1968). Special Wright number. Contains the excellent articles by James A. Emanuel and Cecil Brown cited herein.

New Letters 38 (December 1971). Special Wright number. Includes interesting articles by Margaret Walker Alexander ("Richard Wright") and Morris Dickstein ("Wright, Baldwin, Cleaver").

RAY, DAVID, and FARNSWORTH, ROBERT M., eds. *Richard Wright: Impressions and Perspectives*. Ann Arbor: University of Michigan Press, 1973. Reprint of the December 1971 issue of *New Letters*.

REDDING, J. SAUNDERS. "The Alien Land of Richard Wright." In *Soon, One Morning: New Writing of American Negroes*. Ed. Herbert Hill. New York: Knopf, 1963, pp. 50-59. Wright cut his roots by leaving America.

REILLY, JOHN M. "Richard Wright: An Essay in Bibliography." *Resources for American Literary Study* 1 (1971): 131-80. Very useful annotated bibliography of works about Wright.

______. ed. *Richard Wright: The Critical Reception*. New York: Burt Franklin, 1978. Contemporary critical reviews.

RICKLES, MILTON and PATRICIA. *Richard Wright*. Austin: Steck-Vaughn, 1970. Introductory pamphlet.

SCOTT, NATHAN A., JR. "The Dark and Haunted Tower of Richard Wright." *Graduate Comment* 7 (July 1965): 93-99. Crucial essay; frequently reprinted. "The astonishing thing that it [*Native Son*] finally does is to offer a depraved and inhuman beast as the comprehensive archetypal image of the American Negro."

SIEGEL, PAUL N. "The Conclusion of Richard Wright's *Native Son*." *Publications of the Modern Language Association of America* 89 (May 1974): 517-23. A not completely convincing attempt to reinterpret the ending.

Studies in Black Literature 1 (Autumn 1970). Special Wright number. Includes a useful survey of Wright's poetry by Michel Fabre, "The Poetry of Richard Wright."

TURNER, DARWIN T. "*The Outsider*: Revision of an Idea." *College Language Association Journal* 12 (June 1969): 310-21. *The Outsider* as a revision of *Native Son*.

WEBB, CONSTANCE. *Richard Wright: A Biography*. New York: G. P. Putnam's Sons, 1968. This first biography contains much factual information but is inadequate in many ways.

WEITZ, MORRIS. *Philosophy of the Arts*. Cambridge, Mass.: Harvard University Press, 1950. Bigger represents the tragedy of modern man, who can find autonomy only through violence.

Index

Abbott's Monthly Magazine, 26
Adams, Henry, 44
Alger, Horatio, 21, 26, 171
American Writers' Congress, 33
Aswell, Edward, 36
Atlantic Monthly, 37
Attaway, William: *Blood on the Forge*, 26, 58
Aunt Addie, 22, 23
Aunt Jody, 20
Aunt Maggie, 19, 20, 51

Baker, Houston A., Jr., 46, 95
Baldwin, James, 48, 50, 55, 66, 99, 107, 160, 161; "Everybody's Protest Novel," 107; *Go Tell It on the Mountain*, 99, 108; "Many Thousands Gone," 90, 107
Barrett, Elizabeth, 20
Barthelme, Donald, 106
Barth, John, 106
Beauvoir, Simone de, 109
Beckett, Samuel: *Molloy*, 158
Black Renaissance, 41, 175
Blake, William, 109
Bluebeard, 19
Brewer, Clinton, 121
Brown, Cecil M., 38
Browning, Robert, 20: "Childe Roland to the Dark Tower Came," 157
Burns, Ben, 51

Camus, Albert: *The Stranger*, 158
Cayton, Horace R., 39
Cleaver, Eldridge, 55, 79, 86, 127, 135, 161-64; *Soul on Ice*, 78, 160
Coleridge, Samuel Taylor, 159
Communist party, 23, 27, 32, 33, 34, 37, 49, 67, 75, 84, 85, 90, 114, 115, 116, 120, 137
Conrad, Joseph, 26
Cooper, James Fenimore, 85, 151
Crane, Stephen, 26, 126
Crime International, 52
Cruse, Harold: *The Crisis of the Negro Intellectual*, 72
Cullen, Countee, 48

Daily Worker, 35, 37
Davis, Frank Marshall, 34
Dickstein, Morris, 98
Dos Passos, John, 26, 30
Dostoevsky, Fyodor, 26, 106, 119; *Notes from Underground*, 157
Douglass, Frederick, 41, 44
Dreiser, Theodore, 26, 80, 126
DuBois, W.E.B., 39; *The Souls of Black Folk*, 141
Dumas, Alexandre, 154

Eliot, T.S.: *The Waste Land*, 61
Ellison, Ralph, 24, 35, 46, 99, 107, 108; *Invisible Man*, 25, 55, 83, 99, 114, 116, 157, 158
En-Lai, Chou, 145

Fabre, Michel: *The Unfinished Quest of Richard Wright*, 21
Fanon, Frantz: *The Wretched of the Earth*, 56
Farrell, James T., 34
Ferenzci, Sandor: *Sunday Neuroses*, 121
Fitzgerald, F. Scott: *The Great Gatsby*, 171
Frank, Waldo: *Our America*, 58
Franklin, Benjamin, 44, 171
Frazier, E. Franklin, 39, 40, 138
Freud, Sigmund: *Totem and Taboo*, 121
Frings, Ketti, 52

Garvey, Marcus, 57
Granny (maternal grandmother), 22
Green, Paul, 37
Guggenheim Fellowship, 36

Hallam, Arthur Henry, 20
Harlem Renaissance, 41, 175
Hawthorne, Nathaniel, 46, 86
Hearst, William Randolph, 37
Heeris, Bente, 53
Hegel, G.W.F., 119
Heidegger, Martin, 109, 119
Hemingway, Ernest, 46, 57
Herskovits, Melville, 40, 138
Himes, Chester, 48
Howe, Irving, 107, 108; "Black Boys and Native Sons," 108
Hugo, Victor: *Les Misérables*, 157
Husserl, Edmund, 119

Illinois Federal Writers' Project, 27
International Literature, 28

James, Henry, 46, 106
Jaspers, Karl, 119
Jeffers, Lance, 95-96
Jim Hill Public School, 21
Johnson, Fenton, 34
John Reed Club, 27, 32, 33, 34, 84
Joyce, James, 25; *Ulysses*, 54

Kafka, Franz: *The Trial*, 158
Kierkegaard, Soren, 109, 119

Lawrence, D.H., 151
Left Front, 28, 32, 33

McCall, Dan, 74, 158
Marvell, Andrew, 61
Marxism, 27, 35, 36, 72, 93
Meadman, Dhimah Rose (first wife), 36
Meier, August and Elliott Rudwick: *From Plantation to Ghetto*, 39
Melville, Herman: *Benito Cereno*, 108, 170-71
Mencken, H.L.: *Prejudices*, 25; *A Book of Prefaces*, 25
Moss, Bess, 47
Moss, Mrs., 47

Nehru, Jawaharlal, 146
New Caravan, The, 34
New Challenge, 28, 35
New Masses, 28, 30, 34, 164
Newtons, the, 36
Nietzsche, Friedrich, 119
Nixon, Robert, 101
Nkrumah, Kwame, 139, 140, 141, 154
Norris, Frank, 80, 126

Padmore, George, 48
Partisan Review, 31, 107
Plato: *The Republic*, 159
Poe, Edgar Allan, 26, 86, 129
Poindexter, David, 67
Poplar, Ellen (second wife), 36, 38, 48
Powell, Adam Clayton, 146
Pushkin, Alexander, 154
Pynchon, Thomas, 106

Redding, Saunders, 98
Reynolds, Paul, 37, 132
Robinson, Bob, 67
Rosskam, Edwin, 37, 39

Sablonière, Margrit de, 50, 52
Sapin, Louis: *Papa Bon Dieu*, 51
Sartre, Jean-Paul, 49, 67, 109
Sawyers, the, 35-36
Schwartzmann, Victor, 52, 53
Scottsboro boys, 85
Scott, Nathan A., Jr., 107; "The Dark and Haunted Tower of Richard Wright," 108
Seventh-Day Adventism, 22
Smith-Robinson Public School, 21
Socialist Realism, 30
Southern Register, 21
Stein, Gertrude, 50
Stowe, Harriet Beecher, 78

Tanner, Tony: *City of Words*, 117
Tennyson, Alfred, 20
Tolstoy, Leo, 26
Toomer, Jean: *Cane*, 39

Uncle Clark, 20
Uncle Hoskins, 19, 20

Wagner, Jean: *Black Poets of the United States*, 20
Walker, Margaret, 34, 38
Washington, Booker T., 56, 75; *Up from Slavery*, 138
Webb, Constance, 67, 123
Welles, Orson, 37
Wheatley, Phillis, 154
Wilde, Oscar: *The Ballad of Reading Gaol*, 121
Wilsons, the, (maternal grandparents), 19
Wirth, Louis, 39
Wittenberger, Jan, 84
Wright, Ella (mother), 17, 18, 20, 26
Wright, Julia (daughter), 36
Wright, Leon (brother), 18, 20, 26
Wright, Nathan (father), 17, 18, 25
Wright, Rachel (daughter), 49
Wright, Richard
  WORKS:
  American Hunger, 37, 53
  "American Hunger," 37
  "Between the World and Me," *31-32*, 67, 154
  Black Boy, 18, 19, 21, 22, 23, 37, 38, 39, 40, 41, *43-48*, 53, 57, 62, 63, 77, 83, 88, 109, 113, 119, 120, 130, 137, 138, 140, 166, 171, 174
  "Black Hope," 37
  Black Power, 50, 52, 69, *137-42*, 144, 149, 154, 168
  "Blueprint for Negro Writing," 35
  "Cesspool," 34
  Color Curtain, The, 51, 118, *142-47*
  Eight Men, 52, 53, 125, 128, *156-73*; "Big Black Good Man," 51, *160-64*; "Man, God Ain't Like That. . .," 70, *168-71*; "Man of All Work," 166-68; "The Man Who Killed a Shadow," 164-66; "The Man Who Lived Underground," 37, 77, 110, 113, *156-60*, 164; "The Man Who Saw the Flood," 164; "The Man Who Was Almost a Man," 156; "The Man Who Went to Chicago," 27, 113, *171-73*
  'Hearst Headline Blues," *30*, 88
  "How 'Bigger' Was Born," 95
  "I Have Seen Black Hands," *28*, 39, 154
  "I Tried to Be a Communist," 32, 37, 116
  "Island of Hallucinations," 51, 52, 126, *132-36*
  "Law of a Father, The," 53
  Lawd Today, 26, 34, 53, *54-62*, 63, 71, 110, 119, 123, 132
  "Leader Man," 52
  "Little Sister," 36
  Long Dream, The, 24, 51, 52, *126-32*
  "Melody Limited," 37
  Native Son, 18, 23, 30, 36, 37, 38, 44, 49, 50, 53, 54, 60, 62, 63, 68, 71, 72, 77, *78-108*, 109, 110, 113, 114, 117, 119, 120, 123, 131, 137, 157, 159, 164, 166, 174
  Outsider, The, 26, 44, 48, 49, 50, 56, 58, 88, *109-21*, 137, 157
  Pagan Spain, 139, 140, *147-49*
  "Red Leaves of Red Books," 28, *30-31*
  Savage Holiday, 50, 109, 119, *121-26*, 137
  "Silt" ("The Man Who Saw the Flood"), 164
  "Spread Your Sunrise," 28
  "Superstition," 26, 27
  Twelve Million Black Voices, 37, *38-43*, 45, 46, 47, 48, 67, 164
  Uncle Tom's Children, 35, 36, 57, *62-77*, 128, 174; "Big Boy Leaves Home," 34, *63-67*, 69, 77, 88, 110, 113, 125, 128; "Bright and Morning Star," 34, 62, *75-76*, 77; "Down by the Riverside," *67-69*, 70, 77, 164; "The Ethics of Living Jim Crow" *62-63*, 77; "Fire and Cloud," 35, 41, *71-75*, 76, 77; "Long Black Song," *69-71*, 77
  "Voodoo of Hell's Half Acre, The," 21
  "We of the Streets," 28, *29-30*

"What You Don't Know Won't Hurt You," 27
White Man, Listen!, 51, 52, 118, *150-55*, 168, 170
X, Malcolm, 26, 41, 44